Emotional Intelligence and Nonprofit Leadership Strategies

"EI competencies and leadership strategies must be developed, learned and mastered by 21st-century leaders whether in for-profit or nonprofit organizations."

Dr. Emmanuel A. Peter

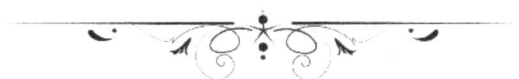

A DESCRIPTIVE INQUIRY INTO THE NONPROFIT LEADERS' PERCEPTIONS ABOUT EMOTIONAL INTELLIGENCE AND LEADERSHIP

By

Dr. Emmanuel A. Peter

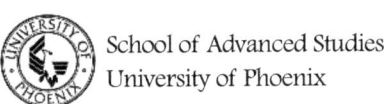

Bill Stokes, DBA

Betty Ahmed, DBA

Thomas Mosby, Ed.D

School of Advanced Studies
University of Phoenix

American Journal *of* Transformational Leadership

Proapt
ProQuest Dissertations
ProQuest Databases

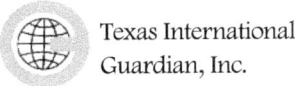
Texas International
Guardian, Inc.

Cover design and book design by Anthony Obi Ogbo,
***Production** by International Guardian*
Publishing: American Journal of Transformational Leadership

This book is a reproduction of studies based on a Dissertation presented
Emmanuel A. Peter in partial fulfillment of the requirements for the degree
Doctor of Management in Organizational Leadership
Research Study Supervision
Bill Stokes, DBA
Betty Ahmed, DBA
Thomas Mosby, Ed.D

Research Study Approval
William C. Beck II, PhD
Academic Dean, School of Advanced Studies,
University of Phoenix

DEDICATION

This dissertation is dedicated first and foremost to my Lord and Savior Jesus Christ the one who gave me power and wisdom to carry out this research project. The scripture says, "Beware lest you say in your heart, my power and the might of my hand gotten me this wealth. You shall remember the Lord your God, for it is he who gives power to get wealth" *(Deuteronomy, 8: 17-18 ESV)*. The study is also dedicated to my parent Elder. and Mrs. Abraham Peter, who nurtured and trained me to be who I am today. Finally, the dissertation is dedicated to my wife Lady Hephzibah and my children Ubong-Abasi, Dorothy, and Amen, who forfeited their comfort, devotion, and fatherly care during this research.

APPRECIATION

The completion of this dissertation could not have been possible without the outstanding contributions of some notable personalities. The input of the Almighty God in the success of this research study cannot be taken for granted. There were times when the process was getting tougher, but the advice of the alumni members in Phoenix-Connect about prayer and diligence kept me going. I will use this medium to acknowledge and appreciate the tireless and selfless assistance of my committee chair Dr. William Stokes, the committee members Dr. Betty Ahmed and Dr. Thomas Mosby. Their honesty, painstaking, and goodwill made this to happen. The contributions of my wife, Lady Hephzibah, and my children Ubong-Abasi, Dorothy, and Amen cannot be forgotten. Particularly, my wife was the editor-in-chief of the project, she typed and also gave all the moral and spiritual supports. Ubong-Abasi, thank you for your patience, I will now have time to pay attention to you and play with you as you always wanted. Dorothy and Amen, we now have all the time in the world to have a fun time with each other. The contribution of my doctoral colleagues I met during this journey cannot be ignored. I will use this medium to appreciate Dr. Darlington Emenike your passionate used of "Ontological and Epistemological" perspectives charged me up to study harder. Dr. Ogbo, your passionate used of the grammar "Dovetail," inspired me so much. Dr. John D'Ascenzo your extraordinary diligence and attention to details inspired me a great deal. Dr. Lisamarie Akinson, your simplicity, and confidence towards the research work inspired me immensely. There are thousands of other supporters I cannot but mention some such as Dr. Joyce Lewis, who emerged from no way to give helping hands to the success of this study. The editing assistance and encouragement of Doyin Muritala is also appreciated. Also, the spiritual and moral supports of Apostle Chibundu Anene cannot be taken for granted. My spiritual father, Pastor Emmanuel Olagunju also assisted spiritually and morally. My colleagues in the GIMF (Global Interdenominational Ministers Fellowship) such as Pastor Chile, Pastor Eddie, Pastor, Sam, Pastor Richard, Apostle Funsho, and a host of others also made a tremendous impact on the success of this research. The moral and academic supports of Dr. Femi, Dr. Ogunnika, Dr. Richard, and Dr. Birch is also very much appreciated. Finally, the contributions of my parent presently in Nigeria, Mr. and Mrs. Abraham Peter who trained, nurtured, and set the pace for me to aim high to the extent of becoming a doctor cannot be trivialized.

-Dr. Emmanuel A. Peter

ABSTRACT

The purpose of this qualitative descriptive study was to explore the perceptions of the NPO leaders about the value of EI
(Emotional Intelligence) on leadership strategies in the City of
Richmond, Virginia. The research problem was the perceptions
of the NPO leaders about the value of EI on leadership strategies in Richmond Virginia was unknown. The need to examine
the NPO leaders' perceptions about EI stemmed from the paradigm shift from cognitive intelligence to EI. Fourteen participants were selected using Seidman's three phase interviews.
The study population was the faith-based and non-faith-based
leaders in the US with samples drawn from NPO leaders in the
City of Richmond, Virginia. The 14 participants were engaged
in in-depth interviews (Seidman's Phase Two), and the data
were analyzed using the NVivo10. The analyzed data resulted
in the emergence of five themes. (a) NPO leaders' perceptions
about the term EI. (b) The leadership atmosphere of organizations in the 21stcentury is sensitive and volatile. (c) The NPO
leaders practice short walking away from the place of stress as
a coping strategy. (d) The NPO leaders practice self-control

with team members to manage conflict and (e) The NPO leaders practice respect for team members for team harmony. The study findings indicated 29% of the participants demonstrated conceptual EI perceptions, while 64% showed practical EI awareness. The remaining 7% expressed moderate or low perceptions of EI. The overall study findings indicated sound EI perceptions among the NPO leaders in Richmond, Virginia.

Table of Contents

TABLE OF CONTENTS

V

Table of Contents

Table of Contents

LIST OF TABLES

LIST OF FIGURES

Chapter 1
Introduction

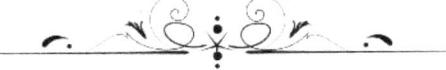

EI may be the answer to most of the emotional issues faced by managers of organizations (Laub, 2011). Temperamental conduct of leaders brings shame and anxiety to the organization and the society as a whole (Laub, 2011).

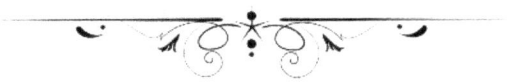

The major scandals that rocked Enron and WorldCom more than a decade ago; and other rotating circles of leadership crisis across sectors, heightened the quest for emotionally intelligent and responsible leadership (Prandini, Vervoort, & Barthelmess, 2012). The leadership need in for-profit organizations may be high, but Grandy (2013) lamented the greater leadership crisis in nonprofit organizations (NPOs). Kahnweiler (2013) predicted severe leadership shortfalls globally in nonprofit agencies. Kahnweiler's prediction remained the most significant challenge of NPOs in the 21-century (Kahnweiler, 2013). Hsieh and Chen (2011) stated the ability of a leader to provide the vision and direction for the success of the business depends on the managerial acuity. Hahn, Sabou, Toader, and Radulscu (2012) agreed with Hsieh and Chen (2011) in linking the leadership effectiveness of leaders to emotional competencies.

Emotional intelligence (EI) represents a variety of mental capabilities and skills that guide a person's power to manage the demand and stress of the environment (Sakiru, Enoho, Kareem, & Abdulahi, 2013). EI can also be defined as the ability to discern one's emotions and the emotions of others, and to use the information to connect, communicate, and influence others (Trautmann, Maher, & Motley, 2007). Colfax, Rivera, and Perez (2010) narrowed the description of a person's EI to possessing common-sense. Similarly, George, Goethals, Allison, and David (2014) described EI as the new collective wisdom. According to Kewalramani, Agrawal, and Rastogi (2015), the scientific understanding of EI enhances the training of one's emotional skills for productive and fulfilling living.

Hahn et al. (2012) stated the concept of EI attracted much recognition as a fundamental factor for managerial effectiveness. George et al. (2014) supported Hahn et al. (2012) by stating EI is a crucial component of leadership effectiveness. The complex leadership environment of the 21st century was critical in exploring the EI perceptions of NPO leaders about the value of EI on leadership (Austin-Roberson, 2009; Cheverton, 2007). The current high demand for EI leaders globally and the importance of emotional skills in the direction of 21-century organizations was also important in embarking on this study (Ross, 2012).

Background

The volatile leadership environment of the 21st-century caused by the presence of more knowledgeable and sensitive workforce suggests the relevance of EI in organizations' leadership (Hickman, 2010). Neera, Anjanee, and Shoma (2010) stated illiteracy in the 21st-century would not mean the inability to read and write, but the inability to learn, "unlearn, and relearn." (p. 21). The leadership of organizations in the current millennium may not succeed effectively with the continued application of the traditional, autocratic, hierarchical, and bureaucratic leadership style that was common in the past (Hickman, 2010). According to Manolis, Chan, Finkelstein, Stephens, Nelson, Grant and Dombeck (2009), new leadership models focus on collaboration, shared leadership, group leadership, and adequate recognition of the workforce.

The incessant reports of misconducts, intolerance, and misbehaviors by some leaders, caused ineffective leaders be categorized incompetent, rigid, intemperate, corrupt, insular, and evil (Hickman, 2010). The categorization of incompetent leaders was the result of extensive leadership research in hundreds of for-profit and NPOs. Ingram and Cangemi (2012) maintained managers have the responsibility to control their state of mind and the state of mind of employees whether convenient or not. Khalili (2013) maintained possession of EI is higher in value than the possession of mathematical and technological skills for the leadership of the 21st-century or-

ganizations. According to George et al. (2014), EI is more
valuable for organizational leadership than cognitive proficiencies.

EI may be the answer to most of the emotional issues faced
by managers of organizations (Laub, 2011). Temperamental
conduct of leaders brings shame and anxiety to the organization and the society as a whole (Laub, 2011). According to
Goleman, Boyatzis and Mckee (2013), a dissonant leader do
not only dispirit the followers but caused them to burn out
and send them packing. The need to explore the EI perceptions of NPO leaders about the value of EI on leadership was
crucial. Also, the linkage of EI to the success of the leaders of
for-profit agencies asserted by many scholars (George et al.,
2014); was the driving force for exploring similar link among
NPO leaders. The next section will be used to examine the
general and concrete problem of this study.

Statement of the Problem

Meyer and Taylor (2013) defined NPO as any privately
owned establishment offering beneficial assistance to the
public at no cost. The NPOs occupy important facets of the
American economy because they encompass a minimum of
1.6 million formal entities and surpasses the number of informal, start-up groups or businesses. In 2010, the NPOs contributions of services and products added $779 billion to the
gross domestic product (GDP) of the U.S. (Urban Institute,
2012). Grandy (2013) stated the success and continuation of
NPOs would require robust and committed leadership. Despite the value of NPOs to U.S economy, the not for the profit
motive of NPOs caused its leadership aspect remain in sham-
ble (Cheverton, 2007). According to Cheverton (2007), the

4

nonprofit sector is still wrestling today with finding meaning and creating a standard for itself, more than focusing on leadership and performance.

The general business problem was the lack of emotionally competent leadership among the nonprofit sector resulting in high rate of fraud and scandals globally among the industry leaders (Prandini, Vervoort, & Barthelmess, 2012; Ross, 2011). The problem persisted despite several scholarly and business reports linking EI to leadership effectiveness (Goleman et al., 2013; George et al., 2014; Rajah, Song, & Arvey, 2011; Sadri, 2012). According to (Trautmann et al., 2007), the search criteria for candidate recruitment in the 21st-century are no longer on the cognitive intelligent, but EI. Research carried out at AT&T, reveals managers with high EI were 20 times more productive than those with low EI (Bradberry & Greaves, 2009). A study conducted by the Carnegie Institute of Technology reveals 85% of a person's productivity is due to emotional alertness or human engineering, personality and ability to communicate, negotiate, and lead. Only 15% is due to the intelligent quotient (Forbes Insights, 2012; Hahn et al., 2012).

The specific business problem was the perceptions of the NPO leaders about the value of EI on leadership strategies in Richmond Virginia was unknown resulting in the training programs decision dilemmas for the sector (Gibelman & Gelman, 2001; Schoenhaus, 2002). According to Grandy (2013), leadership in NPOs is particularly complex and requires responsible leadership. Grandy (2013) maintained leadership of NPOs requires a diverse range of skills and abilities some of which include a high tolerance for ambiguity, advocacy, fundraising, and motivating the workforce. Gibelman and

Gelman (2001) stated the need for new, trained, and committed board members matched with the need for better staff. A research study conducted by Grandy (2013) found emotional and social competencies (e.g. inspirational, transparency) of NPO leaders positively affected their satisfaction. Several EI researchers noted that training programs can be initiated to assist leaders to cope with work-related stress (Jee Young, 2011).

Purpose of the Study

The purpose of this qualitative descriptive study was to explore and examine the perceptions of the NPO leaders about the value of EI on leadership strategies in the City of Richmond, Virginia. Several studies established the positive impact of EI on leadership strategies (Abdul & Ehiobuche, 2011; Bradberry & Greaves, 2009; Goleman et al., 2013; Hahn et al., 2012; Joseph & Newman, 2010; Sadri, 2012; Steven, 2010). For the purpose of the present study, qualitative descriptive inquiry design was used to explore and examine the participants' experiences or perceptions. Seidman's in-depth interviews process was applied to investigate the thought processes of NPO leaders about the value of EI on leadership strategies (Guteng, 2005; Seidman, 2013).

The adoption of qualitative approach facilitated the collection of rich and detailed data, which captures the respondents' experiences and offer a context for the conduct of the participants (Leedy & Ormrod, 2010). The choice of qualitative descriptive inquiry design was expedient because of the need to describe the participants' experiences in details. According to Purpose of Research (2015), most often, descriptive inquiry provide sufficient information about the phenomenon because

6

of it full descriptive capacity. The goals of a qualitative researcher are to explore and generate sufficient knowledge to
lead to understanding or explanation (Davis & Mentzer,
2006). Sadri (2012) stated since the introduction of the concept of EI; several researchers linked EI to leadership effectiveness mostly in for-profit organizations. The direction of
NPOs was left behind in related studies. The study covered
two main types of NPOs (Faith-Based & Non-Faith-Based)
(Meyer & Taylor, 2013). The next section will be used to discuss the significance of the problem.

Significance of the Problem

Significance of the problem to scholarship. Findings from
the present qualitative descriptive study were anticipated to
benefit scholars, educators, and any person in the academic
sector. The results of the doctoral research may contribute to
filling the existing knowledge gap on the link between EI and
leadership in NPOs. Literature so far reviewed revealed
plethora of research on EI and leadership mainly in the for-
profit sector. The research includes the history of EI and organizational leadership attributed to (Bar-On, 1997; Goleman,
2004; Mayer, Salovey, & Caruso, 2002). Current scholarship
on EI was also found such as (Abdul & Ehiobuche, 2011;
Colfax et al., 2010; Goleman et al., 2013; George et al., 2014;
Polychroniou, 2009; Sadri, 2012; Shahhossien et al., 2012,
Wren, 2013).

Significance of the study to future research. The lack of
adequate information about the topic leading to the adoption
of descriptive inquiry made the present research a crucial
groundwork for future research. According to Purpose of Research (2015), usually, descriptive researcher tends to address

new problems with little or no previous research. The descriptive inquiry is an initial inquiry, which forms the groundwork for a more conclusive inquiry (Purpose of Research, 2015). Findings from the present research may assist the future researcher to conduct a more conclusive research about the value of EI on the leadership of NPOs.

Presently, only a handful of EI and leadership literature are found on NPOs (Grandy, 2013). The novelty of the concept of EI sparked arguments among the business and scholarship communities. Example, researchers are arguing that the linkage of EI to leadership advocated by Goleman was not verified by peer review (Sadri, 2012). Some described the claims of Goleman (2004) about EI and leadership as pop psychology (Abdul & Ehiobuche 2011). Proponents of EI maintained EI is valuable than cognitive intelligence (Sadri, 2012). Findings from this study may set a groundwork for solving the existing controversies about EI concept.

Significance of the problem to leadership. The study result may assist for-profit and NPO training institutions in the design of leadership program and courses. The study result may also help human resources department of companies in selecting candidates with EI competencies for employment purposes (Trautmann et al., 2007). The research study may help policy makers to draw leadership plan that may help future leaders in NPOs. The result of the study may proffer solution to emotions related leadership problems in NPOs (Buys & Rothman, 2010; Larin, Benson, Wessel, & Williams, 2011). According to Buys and Rothman (2010), burnout issues have been major problems for individuals, companies, and health agencies in the past 20 years.

Colfax et al. (2010) posited the 21st-century businesses

prefer leaders with high EI to leaders with high intelligent quotient because of the vast studies linking EI to leadership success. Based on the change of focus from cognitive skills to personality and social skills in the leadership domain (George et al., 2014), the result may help leaders to reappraise their leadership styles. The study result may help any person in a leadership position evaluate emotional state and skills for leadership and everyday living. The next section will be used to discuss the nature of the study.

Nature of the Study

Following a field test validating the interview questions. Participants soliciting emails and telephone calls were sent to NPO leaders in Richmond. The solicitation was based on purposive sampling of 14 participants (Patton, 1990). The study participants were preselected using the first phase of Seidman's interview process (Seidman, 2013). The right sample size of the study was determined through data saturation (Kerr, 2010). According to Ives Tay Assoc CIPD BBA (2014), data saturation is the continuous gathering of information until theoretical saturation is attained. Theoretical saturation is achieved when no relevant or new insights are emerging from the data gathered (Ives Tay Assoc CIPD BBA, 2014).

Recently, the right number of interviews to attain data saturation has raised contention among scholars. While some argued that three consecutive interviews with no new information revealed lead to saturation; some stated that five or six one-hour interviews result in saturation, some suggested 10, and some suggested 12 interviews (Creswell, 2013; Ives Tay Assoc CIPD BBA, 2014). For the purpose of the current qualitative descriptive study, the data saturation was determined when three consecutive interviews was administered with no new information revealed (Ives Tay Assoc CIPD BBA, 2014). The selected participants acknowledge and signed the informed consent before participation in the study (Qualitative Research Methods, 2015).The first phase of Seidman's interviews addressed the context of the study (EI perceptions) and the professional background of the participants.

The participant's background was explored to ensure they met the study recruitment criteria (Guteng, 2005; Seidman, 2013). The criteria for recruitment for the study centered on possessing basic knowledge of EI, residency in Richmond, basic academic qualification, and leadership experience measured by staff strength and years of leadership. The qualitative research method was used in the study. The qualitative method was appropriate for the current study because it was a more robust approach to understanding the issue under study than quantitative method (Leedy & Ormrod, 2010). According to Leedy and Ormrod (2010), a qualitative study explores the complex nature of phenomena from the point of view of the participants.

Yin (2013) stated qualitative research is designed to explore the differences of complicated human conduct in a particular setting. Quantitative analysis was not adequate, as the focus of this study centered on the experiences and perceptions of the participants, offering no quantitative data to analyze (Steven, 2010). According to Onwuegbuzie and Collins (2010), quantitative study is "a study where the researcher determines what to verify, ask specific, narrow questions, collect numeric data from participants, analyze these number using statistics and conduct an inquiry in an objective manner" (p.39). The use of qualitative inquiry or in-depth interpretive process to harness the experiences of participants may offer adequate result (Onwuegbuzie & Collins, 2010; Patton, 1990).

The closest research method that would have proffered solution to the research problem was a mixed method. According to Onwuegbuzie and Collins (2010), mixed methods combines the quantitative and qualitative research methods together to find a solution to research problems. But the vastness of mixed methods research were disadvantageous to the study because it did not offer enough explorative opportunity needed in the study. According to Leedy and Ormrod (2010), mixed methods researchers divide attention to the quantitative and qualitative strands sequentially or concurrently. The division of attention to two methods at the same time may create a challenge of providing limited attention to the area of high priority (qualitative) (Leedy & Ormrod, 2010).

The phenomenological design could have served the need of the current study. But the research goal goes beyond the narrow focus of exploring the participant's lived experiences done by phenomenological researchers (Leedy & Ormrod, 2010). The qualitative descriptive inquiry design was selected because it offered adequate platform to tackle the research problem. According to Arbnor and Bjerke (2009), the views of the researcher, the perspective of the study problem, and the study questions, determines the selection of the methodology.

In other words, Arbnor and Bjerke (2009) implied that the nature of the problem determines the solution process. Purpose of Research (2015) defined descriptive inquiry as an effort to examine and explore the participants' experiences by describing the event in details, supplying the missing information for adequate comprehension. According to Purpose of Research (2015), most often, descriptive inquiry provide sufficient information about the phenomenon because of it full descriptive capacity. Because of the lack of information about the value of EI on the leadership of NPOs, a careful description of the event may reveal more details about the participants' perceptions.

The first best alternative to the selected design was a case study. The Case study was attractive because of its power to examine cases using multiple sources of data (De Weed-Nederhof, 2001). But the independent, holistic, and the descriptive capacity of descriptive inquiry outmatched case study design. According to Schwandt (2015), descriptive research cut across a plethora of philosophical and methodological ideas drawn from the interpretative tradition. The explanatory family includes among others; semiotics, cultural studies, ethnography, ethnomethodology, hermeneutics, and phenomenology (Schwandt, 2015). Sandelowski (2000) maintained that qualitative descriptive inquirer's goal is to describe the event in a complete summation. Lambert and Lambert (2012) also supported the uniqueness and independence of descriptive inquiry, adding that the design is the least theoretical dependence than all others.

The second best alternative design for the study was grounded theory. Despite the similarity of methodology, grounded theory was rejected because the primary objective of the research practitioner was not to build theory. Grounded theory is a qualitative study design that involves developing a theory based on the data collected instead of collecting data after a theory has already formed (Purpose of Research, 2015). Although the present research may lay groundwork for theory building, the descriptive power and the holistic worldview of descriptive inquiry made grounded theory design inadequate for the current study (Schwandt, 2015).

The best alternative design for this dissertation was the narrative inquiry. But the narrative inquiry was rejected because the researcher's goal was not to reduce the research to mere storytelling as practiced by narrative inquirers (Creswell, 2013). Although, the collection of stories, reporting the experiences of individuals, and chronologically ordering the meaning of those experiences could add a qualitative rigor to the study; but descriptive inquiry combined rigor, thick description and flexibility to the study (Creswell, 2013). Creswell (2013) also stated an aspect of story-telling, a great feature of narrative inquiry is already embedded in the descriptive research design adopted in this dissertation.

Descriptive research was also found to be more comprehensive than other qualitative models because it describes the participants' experiences as expressed in a lived and told stories a feature of phenomenology and narrative inquiry (Creswell, 2012). Magilvy and Thomas (2009) asserted the thick description of the participants' experiences afforded the researcher a rich platform for better comprehension of the respondents' view point. Above all, the drafting of interview questions based on the hypothetical future situation could not have been properly addressed using narrative inquiry than the descriptive one. The descriptive ramifications of the adopted design were the right fit in dealing with the research question and the purpose of this study (Arbnor & Bjerke, 2009).

The second and third phases of Seidman's interview

process was applied in the collection of the study data. The interview was conducted face-to-face or through Skype and the telephone. The second step of Seidman's interviews enabled participants to reconstruct the details of their experiences or perceptions within the context using open-ended questions (Guteng, 2005). The third phase allowed participants to reflect on their experiences and review their interview transcripts (Seidman, 2015). The interview transcription was done using Microsoft words and digital voice recorder.

In-depth interviews are important in the qualitative study because it results in an advanced knowledge of the social context of people's experience (Granot et al., 2012). A computer software, NVivo10 was used for data coding and categorization. The next section will be used to discuss the research question for the study. The relevance of the research question to the study cannot be over-stressed as it attempts to find a solution to the research problem of the study.

Research Questions

For the purposes of the present study, two research questions (RQ1) and (RQ2) were examined.

RQ1: What are the perceptions of NPO leaders concerning the value of EI on leadership strategies in Richmond Virginia? The purpose of the question was to explore the perceptions of NPO leaders about the value of EI on their leadership strategies. The answer to the research question helped in articulating the current position of NPO leaders in terms of emotional awareness and their leadership strategies (George et al., 2014). The answer to the research question also helped in bridging the knowledge gap in the current area of study. McMurray, Pirola-Merlo, Sarr Notos, and Islam (2010) main-

14

tained while there are many research studies in the for-profit sector, the nonprofit sector lags behind in the research dealing with EI and leadership strategies. The second research question for the study was:

RQ2: What are the perceptions of the faith-based NPO leaders compared to that of the non-faith-based NPO leaders concerning the value of EI on their leadership strategies in Richmond Virginia? The purpose of this question was to examine the differences in opinion if any about the value of EI on leadership among the two subdivisions of the NPOs. The need to examine the differences was unconnected with the asserted over-spiritualization of the employee discipline among the faith-based NPO leaders (McMurray et al., 2010). See Appendix B for interview questions. The next section will be used to discuss the conceptual framework of the study.

Theoretical Framework

The purpose of this section is to explore the prior knowledge of the research practitioner about the concepts of the study (Cepeda & Martin, 2005). In the absence of the conceptual framework, the research practitioner may be in the dilemma of offering meaningless and unfounded description about the study (Meyer, 2001). Previous research on EI by (Goleman, 2004; Salovey & Mayer, 2004), Big Five personality traits theory by (Saxena, 2014) and leadership theories by (Hamlin, 2005; Wren, 2013) provided the conceptual framework for the present study.

The theory of EI is a relatively new theoretical construct in behavioral sciences literature (Askhanansy & Dashborough, 2003). The history of EI traced to Thorndike (1920), identified social intelligence as the potential to interact with people in a social environment (Law, Wong, & Song, 2004). Riggio

15

and Reichard (2008) stated that the idea of EI was first discussed officially by Salovey and Mayer in (1990) but was expanded by Goleman in (1995). The two traditional theories of EI are the ability-based theory (Salovey & Mayer, 2002), and the mixed model or theory (Bar-On, 1997; Goleman, 2004). For the purpose of this descriptive inquiry, the two traditional EI theories and the leadership theories was discussed as the framework of theories. Other EI theory such as the trait EI theory were discussed at the literature review's section. Also discussed in the literature review were the servant leadership theory, passive avoidance or laissez faire theory and a comparison of the situational and contingency theories.

Ability-Based EI Theory: Sadri (2012) defined EI as "The capacity to reason about emotions, and of emotions to enhance thought" (p. 536). EI also connotes the abilities to recognize emotions, to gain entry and induce feelings in order to aid thinking (Sadri, 2012). Also discussed under EI construct was the capacity to comprehend feelings and mental awareness, and control feelings in order to advance psychological and spiritual development (Joseph & Newman, 2010; Sadri, 2012). Sadri (2012) further stated the intellectual communities widely accept ability-based model.

Gignac (2010) noted ability-based design is homogeneous in nature and is usually measured by psychometric tests example "Mayer-Salovey-Caruso Emotional Intelligence Test" (MSCET) (p. 312). Riggio and Reichard (2008) said the healthiest method to measure EI is the ability model designed by Salovey, Mayer, and Caruso (2002). The contribution of the ability-based model to this dissertation is the model created awareness for leaders to exerise self-consciousness, self-control and exhibit social skills (Gignac, 2010). Emotional skills such as self-discipline helped leaders avoids unwarranted conflicts but maintains sound emotional growth (See Figure 1).

The Mixed Theory of EI: Goleman (2004) defined EI as capacities including the power to be inspired and endure disappointment; the power to regulate feelings; and to "delay gratification." (Sadri, 2012, p.537). According to Goleman (2004), EI also includes the power to control temper and manage stress from overwhelming ability to reason, to be hopeful, and to empathize (Sadri, 2012). Goleman's model is classified as a mixed model and is widely celebrated by people in the non-scholastic circles (Joseph & Newman, 2010; Sadri, 2012). The ability to endure disappointment, and manage stress from overwhelming ability to reason, is an essential quality needed by the 21st century's leaders (Ross, 2012).

Goleman's mixed model highlighted four principal EI constructs: (a) Self-awareness: ability to study one's emotion and identify consequences. (b) Self-management involves managing one's emotions and adjusting to dynamic situations.(c) Social awareness the ability to perceive, comprehend, and act to others' emotions while understanding social system. (d) Relationship-management is the ability to motivate, impact and grow while controlling dispute (Abdul & Ehiobuche, 2011; Batool, 2013; Goleman et al., 2013).

Leadership idea is as old as the concept of civilization (Neera et al., 2010). Leadership is also the world oldest preoccupation (Wren, 2013). Scholars, business experts, and business practitioners have attempted to define leadership in various ways (Northhouse, 2015). Northhouse (2015) defined leadership as the capacity to influence others. The major leadership eras: the trait era, the contingency era, and the present era forms the bedrock of leadership theories (Wren, 2013).

The Trait/Great Man Theory: Trait theory based on identifying characteristics that made people efficient leaders. These include factors such as personality, height, class, and age. The concept of trait theory lies on the notion that there are certain standards (appropriate trait/s) that identifies a leader from a non-leader (Faurgier & Woolnough, 2002). According to Neera et al. (2010), great man theories were based on the study of people who were already great. The primary assumption was that leaders are born and not made. The leading proponent of trait model is the Scottish historian Thomas Carlyle during the industrial revolution (Allio, 2010).

Situational Leadership Theory: Situational leadership is a dynamic leadership style where the leader adopts any style according situation. According to Faugier and Woolnough (2002), the most efficient leader does not hold onto one leadership style all the time; instead, change between leadership styles as a different situation may demand different leadership options. Effective leaders adopt different leadership style depending on the proficiency of the companions. For a leader to be efficient, such must identify where the workers are in the advancement spectrum and adopt a leadership style accordingly.

Contingency Leadership Theory: Allio (2013) stated contingency leadership theorists advocated success of a leader depended on the interrelationship of some factors. Namely, (a) work needed performance, (b) the leaders and followers' relationship or connection, and (c) the positional power of the leader. Other factors include the cooperation of the members to work and the ability of the leader to exercise the authority bestowed on him or her (Allio, 2013). Fielder contingency model in Amiri et al. (2010) indicated the efficiency of a group is contingent on leadership style and conducts instead of traits.

Transformational Leadership Theory: Transformational leadership in certain aspects is an extension of transactional leadership (Bottomley et al., 2014), but transformational leaders inspire their followers to perform above what they planned to do and beyond what they could imagine. With the application of motivational and encouragements tools, transformational leaders mostly have committed and satisfied followers. Unlike transactional leaders, transformational leaders empower their followers and attend to their personal development (Hickman, 2010). Because of the predominant use of volunteers in nonprofit organizations such as the focus of this research, there is no doubt that NPOs leaders need to be transformative.

Transactional Leadership Theory: Hickman (2010) defined "transactional leadership" as leadership that transpires when the supervisor recompenses or punishes the follower, according to the member's performance (p. 79). Transactional or exchange theories of leadership emphasize the relationship between a leader and a follower based on mutual exchange, signifying that nothing goes for nothing. Bottomley et al. (2014) stated this style of leadership is usually autocratic, and task oriented. Transactional leaders managed by exception, i.e., changes in management style should not be affected unless there is a problem. They only react when a problem occurs and tend to use negative feedback and punitive measures to staff (Amiri et al., 2010; Faugier & Woolnough, 2002).

The Big Five Personality Theory: The theory of personality is another critical theory that added to the framework of theories of this study. Although EI is not synonymous with personality, Mayer Salovey and Caruso (2002) maintained that being EI is not equivalent to possessing agreeable personality trait; or other personality traits, but EI and personality enhance each other. According to Saxena (2014), personality traits is any mental attributes that enable a person's thinking and behaving in a distinctive and enduring patterns. In 1963, a neuropsychologist, W.I. Norman grouped personality traits into five components tagged the Five Factors Model (FFM) or the Big Five personality traits (Derue, Nahrgang, Wellman, & Humphrey, 2011; MentalHelp.net, 2016; Saxena, 2014).

Among the FFM components are extraversion, agreeableness, conscientiousness, neuroticism and openness to experience (Judge & Bono, 2000; MentalHelp.net, 2016; Saxena, 2014). Over the years, the big FFM has become prominent in the psychological world and has been studies in relation to job performance, job satisfaction, performance motivations, career success in addition to organizational outcomes and other related personality domain (Saxena, 2014). The relevance of the big five model to the leadership of the 21st organizations cannot be overestimated. The components of the big five model independently and collectively enhance leadership effectiveness. The five big five elements are summarized below:

Neuroticism or Emotional Instability. Neuroticism is a personality factor that communicates a person's possibility to be emotional, defensive, or anxious (MentalHelp.net, 2016: Saxena, 2014).

Extraversion. Extraversion is a personality trait that highlights the social-assertiveness, activeness, boldness, energetic, and adventurousness of an individual (Saxena, 2014). According to MentalHelp.net (2016), the extroverts are often action-oriented and mostly experience positive emotions.

Openness to Experience. Openness to experience personality traits is reflective in the divergence of thinking, creativity, imaginative, autonomy, and unconventionality of an individual (Judge & Bono, 2000; MentalHelp.net, 2016; Saxena, 2014).

Agreeableness. Agreeable traits pertain to individuals who are cooperative, trusting, generous, and warm (Judge & Bono, 2000; MentalHelp.net, 2016; Saxena, 2014). According to Saxena (2014), agreeable people are often tender-minded, modest, straightforward, and getting along with people.

Conscientiousness. Conscientious people are success-oriented, deliberate, diligence, responsible, and dependable (Judge & Bono, 2000; MentalHelp.net, 2016; Saxena, 2014). Saxena (2016) noted conscientious people tended to be reliable, goal-focus, disciplined and self-regulated.

Definition of Terms

The following are the definitions of the relevant terms used in this study:

Emotional Intelligence. EI represents a variety of mental capabilities and skills that guides a person's power to manage the demand and stress of the environment (Sakiru, Enoho,

Kareem, & Abdulahi, 2013). EI can also be defined as a person's power to identify and react to intuitions of oneself and the intuitions of others (Tucker, Sojka, Barone, & McCarthy, 2000).

Emotional demands. Refers to the emotional situations that ministers faced in their work in dealing with people. Emotional demands revolve around the excessive and unscheduled nature of NPO leaders' jobs (Buy & Rothmann, 2010).

Leadership strategies. Leadership strategies encompassed the leader's strategic vision or focus such as servant leadership, stewardship, shared leadership or participatory leadership that the leader hope to achieve (De Kluyver, 2012).

Relationship management. Relationship management is the potential to motivate, impact and grow while controlling dispute (Abdul & Ehiobuche, 2011). Relationship management simply entails a person's power to relate tactfully with others.

Self-awareness. Self-awareness entails a person capacity to study his or her emotion and identify consequences (Abdul & Ehiobuche, 2011). Self-awareness connotes the ability of an individual to understand oneself and social boundaries (Goleman et al., 2013).

Self-management. Self-management involves managing one's emotions and adjusting to dynamic situations (Abdul & Ehiobuche, 2011).

Social-awareness. Social-awareness is the capacity to perceive, comprehend, and act to others' emotions while understanding social systems (Abdul & Ehiobuche, 2011).

Assumptions

The assumptions of the study entail the suppositions, presumptions, expectations or speculations guiding the research. The proposed doctoral study based on the following assumptions. The first assumption was the answer of the participants to the interview questions will be reliable, honest, and free from biases. The next assumption was emotional competency or skill of a leader in for-profit and nonprofit organizations is not different (McMurray et al., 2010).

Scope and Limitations

The scope of this study revolved around the study population. According to Creswell (2013), the scope of a study define boundaries and establish the rationale for the study. The study was conducted in the city of Richmond, Virginia. Fourteen participants were interviewed to investigate their EI perceptions about the value of EI on leadership strategies. According to Mason (2010), the participant size for qualitative research ranges from five to 65. Qualified participants were selected from the executive cadre in the organization, such as President, CEO, Senior Pastor, Executive Director, Manager, Associate Pastor, or Assistant Manager; provided the person meet the recruitment requirements. Qualified organizations were NPO (faith-based or non-faith-based), such as church, mosque, schools, hospital, or charities. The selected participants had a minimum of 3 years leadership experience in their respective NPOs in the City of Richmond.

The limitations of a study entail those factors, conditions, or elements which the research practitioner is unable to manipulate (Dusick, 2011). The study was restrained by the following limitations: (a) Leadership challenges in for-profit organizations may not apply to the leadership of NPOs. The reason is the motive of creation and mode of operation in the two sectors are not the same (Cheverton, 2007; Trautman et al., 2007). (b) Because of the voluntary ramification of participation, some volunteers decided not to complete the interview session and may pulled out.

Delimitations

The delimitations of the present study were those elements or factors that the researcher was able to control for effective researching. According to Creswell (2013), delimitations in research studies refers to the restrictions or boundaries that the researcher impose to streamline the scope of the study. This study was limited to the faith-based and non-faith-based NPO leaders with a minimum qualification of a bachelor degree and above. The prospective participants were required to have a bachelor degree equivalent and above. The rationale behind the requirements was to ensure the selected members have basic educational training to be conversant with the concept of EI or EI components, and can differentiate it from personality traits.

The second delimitation was the NPO leaders were required to practice the profession for at least 3 years. The staff strength under the supervision of the faith-based NPOs and non-faith-based leader was required to be a minimum of five workers. The rationale for combining academic ramification and leadership experiences was to ensure leaders do not just have academic qualifications to participate in the study but have no consistent leadership experience.

Chapter Summary

In Chapter 1, the study topic was introduced. The introduction that the major scandals that rocked Enron and World-Com, which heightened the quest for emotionally intelligent and responsible leaders were highlighted (Prandini, Vervoort, & Barthelmess, 2012). The aim of the study was to investigate the EI perceptions of NPO leaders about the value of EI on leadership strategies. The study problem was the perceptions of the NPO leaders about the value of EI on leadership strategies in Richmond Virginia was unknown.

The study result was anticipated to contribute significantly to the wellbeing and development of scholars, leadership, educators, churches leaders, and even family leaders. The study findings were anticipated to help in bridging the knowledge gap in the area of EI and leadership in NPOs. The study result was also expected to help companies in search for emotionally competent leaders. The study questions were also anticipated to assist in finding answer/s to the research problem. Qualitative descriptive study design was selected for the study. The conceptual framework of the study was based on the previous researches on EI by (Goleman, 2004; Mayer & Salovey, 2002), and the leadership studies by Wren (2013). The big five personality factor model also contributed to the framework of theories of the study.

The operational definitions used in the study were also explained. The assumption's that the study participants will be honest highlighted. The limitation of the study hinging on the voluntary ramification of the study was emphasized. The scope of the study that revolves around the study population, delimitation, and participant's qualifications was stressed. The next chapter of the dissertation (Chapter 2) will be used to review the previous literature related to the study. Literature on EI, EI history, EI and leadership, leadership history and theories, leadership challenges, and 21st-century leadership, were examined.

Chapter 2
Literature Review

■ The linkage of EI to job performance confirms the connection of EI to leadership and team development speculated by several scholars (Akins, 2015; Batool, 2013; Goleman et al., 2013).

A literature review is a crucial component of any academic research and contains critical discussions of theory and practical applications related to this dissertation. The purpose of this qualitative descriptive study was to explore and examine the perceptions of the NPO leaders about the value of EI on leadership strategies in the City of Richmond, Virginia. In the current chapter, three primary literature categories that integrate the germinal, and current literature was reviewed. The first literature class presents reviews of the literature on EI. Within the general theme of EI, sub-elements such as the historical overview of EI, EI models, a critical analysis of EI, and EI and leadership was discussed. Also discussed in the first literature class was the big five personality model.

The next category of the review focused on literature on leadership with sub-elements such as the historical overview of leadership, leadership models, leadership challenges, and the 21st-century leadership demands. The third category of the review discussed literature on NPOs. The section included sub-elements such as multiple definitional perspectives of NPOs, a historical overview with a great emphasis on leadership lapses in NPOs. Related research methods and the selected design of the study were also reviewed. The findings of these literature reviews revealed the knowledge gap about the problem investigated by the study. The literature review also assisted in developing and validating the conceptual framework for the study as described in Chapter1.

Title Searches, Articles, Research Documents, and Journals

Several content searches were carried out using the following terms: Social and emotional intelligence, NPOs, non-governmental organizations (NGOs), third sector organizations, leadership, servant leadership, and leadership problems. Other search terms were leadership effectiveness, leadership strategies, leadership theories, transformational leadership, emotional skills, emotional competencies, and EI models. The sources of literature for the present study came from a plethora of scholarly sources. The literature reviewed included theories, definitions, and descriptions of studies relevant to the research question and the study problem. But the primary criteria for the selected sources was the materials were peer-reviewed.

The majority of the literature reviewed for the study were sourced from the University of Phoenix online library. The databases searched were, ProQuest, EBSCOhost, Gale, Pro-Quest digital dissertations for published dissertations from most universities, and the University of Phoenix dissertation database. Other sources were resource books and periodicals from Virginia Commonwealth University (VCU), Internet search engines such as Google scholars and other scholarly resources, such as memos, reports, and others. Table 1 presents a summary of major literature title searches. See Table 1.

Table 1
Summary of Major Literature Title Searches

Topics Reviewed	Peer Reviewed Journals	Websites	Books
Leadership Theories Models	155	21	35
Emotional Intelligence Models	73	37	25
Nonprofit Organizations	121	28	36
Research Methodology	132	25	35

Emotional Intelligence

The idea of EI gained appreciable attention over the past decades and is widely associated with leadership development and performance (Sadri, 2012). EI was defined by scholars using different perspectives. According to Mayer, Salovey, and Caruso (2002), EI is "the ability to reason about emotions, and of emotions to enhance thinking" (p. 535). Goleman (2004) defined EI as capacities including the power to be inspired and endure disappointment. The power to regulate feelings; "delay gratification" control temper; and manage stress from overwhelming ability to reason, to be hopeful, and to empathize (Sadri, 2012, p.537). On-the-other-hand, Polychroniou (2009) defined EI as the capacity of an individual to be aware of his or her instinct and the instinct of others. EI also include the power to differentiate between instincts, and apply the knowledge to direct reasoning and conduct (Akins, 2015).

Historical Overview of EI

The origin of EI was traced to the construct of "social intelligence" pioneered and discussed by "Thorndike" in 1920 (Batool, 2013; Colfax, Rivera, & Perez, 2010, p. 89). Thorndike (1920) defined social intelligence as the power to comprehend and organize individuals to act intelligently in human relationship (Colfax, et al., 2010). Gardner in (1993) extended the multiple intelligence theory to include interpersonal and intrapersonal intelligences (Gardner, 2011). In 1993, Gardner highlighted that social intelligence is a major component of the seven intelligence realms and encompassed individual's interpersonal and intrapersonal bits of intelligence (Chopra & Kanji, 2010; Colfax et al., 2010; Gardner, 2011).

The term EI was first mentioned in the USA by Payne (1983) in a doctoral research, studying the acknowledgement and values of emotion (Hess & Bacigalupo, 2011; Payne, 1983). EI as a concept was first officially presented and discussed by Salovey and Mayer in (1990), but was expanded by

Goleman in (1995), (Goleman, 2004; Riggio & Reichard, 2008). According to Sadri (2012), the construct of EI received full attention and recognition after the publication of Goleman's book titled, Goleman's Emotional Intelligence (1995). Abdul and Ehiobuche (2011) noted prior to Payne's (1983) mentioning of EI in his doctoral thesis; EI had appeared in Leuner (1966). Abdul and Ehiobuche (2011) added EI model also featured in the work of Greenspan before the formal elaboration of the concept by Salovey and Mayer (1990, p. 45). Based on the literature, the concept of EI is known since the mid1960s. The conflicting report about the origin of EI revealed a gap in the literature that needs filling.

Trautman et al. (2007) stated although EI is defined in a variety of ways, the essence of the EI concept remained the emphasis of the researchers. According to Trautmann et al. (2007), the essence of EI is the ability to discern emotions and to use the information to connect, communicate, and influence others. Riggio and Reichard (2008) stated shortage in emotional skills is incriminated to some sorts of abnormal behavior, leading to low level of social and emotional experience that can break down families and other relationships.

Models of Emotional Intelligence

There are two traditional theories of EI. These include the ability-based model (Joseph & Newman, 2010; Salovey & Mayer, 2000), and the mixed model (Bar-On, 1997; Goleman, 2004; Joseph & Newman, 2010). Other models such as the trait model discussed by Abdul and Ehiobuche (2011) was not as general as the two mentioned traditional models. But for the purpose of this dissertation, all the known EI models were worthy to be discussed.

Ability-Based EI Model. Sadri (2012) defined EI as "The capacity to reason about emotions, and of emotions to enhance thought" (p. 536). EI also connotes the abilities to recognize emotions, to gain entry and induce feelings in order to aid thinking (Sadri, 2012). Also discussed under EI construct was the capacity to comprehend feelings and mental awareness, and control feelings in order to advance psychological and spiritual development (Joseph & Newman, 2010; Sadri, 2012). Sadri (2012) further stated the intellectual communities widely accept ability-based model.

Gignac (2010) noted ability-based design is homogeneous in nature and is usually measured by psychometric tests example "Mayer-Salovey-Caruso Emotional Intelligence Test" (MSCET), (p. 312). Riggio and Reichard (2008) said the healthiest method to measure EI is the ability model designed by Salovey, Mayer, and Caruso (2002). The contribution of the ability-based model to this dissertation is the model created awareness for leaders to exercise self-consciousness, self-control and exhibit social skills (Gignac, 2010). Emotional skills such as self-discipline helped leaders avoids unwarranted conflicts but maintains sound emotional growth (See Figure 1).

The Mixed EI Model. Goleman (2004) defined EI as capacities including the power to be inspired and endure disappointment; the power to regulate feelings; and to "delay gratification." (Sadri, 2012, p.537). According to Goleman (2004), EI also includes the power to control temper and manage stress from overwhelming ability to reason, to be hopeful, and to empathize (Sadri, 2012). Goleman's model is classified as a mixed model and is widely celebrated by people in the non-scholastic circles (Joseph & Newman, 2010;

Sadri, 2012).The ability to endure disappointment, and manage stress from overwhelming ability to reason, is an essential quality needed by the 21st century's leaders (Ross, 2012).

Goleman's mixed model highlighted four principal EI constructs: (a) Self-awareness is the ability to study one's emotion and identify consequences. (b) Self-management involves managing one's emotions and adjusting to dynamic situations. (c) Social awareness is the ability to perceive, comprehend, and act to others' emotions while understanding social system. (d) Relationship-management is the ability to motivate, impact and grow while controlling dispute (Abdul & Ehiobuche, 2011; Batool, 2013; Goleman et al., 2013).

Sadri (2012) reported five skills sets of Goleman's mixed model as "self-awareness, self-regulation, motivation, empathy and social skills" (p. 538). Mixed model is measured using Emotional Competency Inventory (ECI) (Akins, 2015; Gignac, 2010). Gignac (2010) stated the ability-based model assessments are highly rated than the self-report assessments of mixed model. According to Gignac (2010), ability-based model do not rely on self-rating and are not vulnerable to socially desirable answers. But, Goleman's mixed model added a crucial dimension to the current study, i.e. empathy and social skills. Leaders with empathy and social skills may understand followers adequately and create a harmonious working relationship (Goleman et al., 2013) (See Figure 1).

Trait EI Model. EI model classified as trait model is very close to personality domain. Trait EI model can be defined as an array of psychological self-recognition or a collection of emotions relating to temperaments and self-awareness, measured through self-rated surveys (Abdul & Ehiobuche, 2011). The model was propounded by a British psychologist Konstantin Petrides (Abdul & Ehiobuche, 2011). EI trait model has to do with the self-awareness of individuals regarding the emotional capabilities and encompasses attitudinal inclinations and self-recognition abilities (Abdul & Ehiobuche, 2011). Unlike the ability-based model that is peer, subordinate, or superordinate rated, trait model like mixed model is self-rated, (Akins, 2015; Hay Group, 2012). Hay Group (2012) stated the newly created 360 edition of mixed model can enable the emotional skills of leaders to be rated by others. Abdul and Ehiobuche (2011) stated that Trait model is measured using "Trait Emotional Intelligence Questionnaire (TEIQue)" (p.53).

In the final analysis, the three models (Trait model, ability-based model, and mixed model), emphasized the need for self-consciousness and self-regulation of leaders. A leader who is not able to have a good grip of his or her emotions may not know when he or she is crossing the emotional boundary. Crossing the psychological boundary may damage the leader's reputation and the corporate image of the organization that may be costly and difficult to rebuild (Laub, 2011). Goleman et al. (2013) maintained a leader that fails in the primal duty of driving emotions in the right path, cannot accomplish any task as it should.

Critical Review of EI

The emergence of the concept of EI has witnessed different schools of thought supporting or opposing the idea. For the benefit of the study, it was imperative to evaluate the credibility or falsity of this crucial and controversial theory. Scholars maintained the extravagant claims of EI by Goleman in his book Goleman's Emotional Intelligence (1995) did not receive the endorsement of the peer review journals. Mayer et al. (2000) described Goleman's EI claims as pop psychology (Abdul & Ehiobuche, 2011).

Gignac (2010) also faulted Goleman's mixed-model of EI by stating the self-reported measures of the model depends on self-rating and are vulnerable to socially undesirable responses. Law et al. (2004) examined all the EI-related scales and concluded that most of the scales had relevant bearings on personality dimensions making EI is an elusive construct. Sadri (2012) found the assumptions of EI transcends boundaries of what a rational description of intelligence should be. Sadri (2012) said although the evaluation of EI signifies sufficient trustworthiness, but the proof of dependability is lacking.

Supporters of the construct of EI have contended EI is different from traditional character traits and general mental ability (GMA). General mental abilities are significant design that can be used to expound various mental and supervisory events (Law et al., 2004). Law et al. (2004) created a new EI scale and showed in addition to the GMAs; EI was a good forecaster of work accomplishment. The linkage of EI to job performance confirms the connection of EI to leadership and team development speculated by several scholars (Akins, 2015; Batool, 2013; Goleman et al., 2013).

According to Mayer, Salovey, and Caruso (2000), EI has fulfilled basic yardsticks establishing it as intelligence type. Daus and Ashkanasy (2003) discovered the ability-based design of EI displays adequate confluence and peculiarity potency to reinforce its affirmation as intelligence class. According to Ashkanasy and Daus (2003), EI represents a personal individuality factor that develop in the course of human existence and can strengthen through orientation or training. According to Akins (2015), Taking public speaking classes, accountability classes, and responsibility classes can also enhance one's EI. Sadri (2012) suggested there are some reasons to be optimistic about the future of EI, but hinted that it is still a long way before EI idea becomes universally appreciated (Sadri, 2012).

Emotional Intelligence and Leadership

Many previous scholars have linked the concept of EI to leadership development. Famous among the scholars is Goleman (1998). Goleman (1998) became so outspoken about EI and leadership reporting that a research conducted at approximately 200 large, global companies demonstrated EI especially at the top-level of an organization is sine qua non to leadership. Goleman concluded if there is a lack of EI, a leader can have a top-of-the-line educational training, insightful mind, and countless stock of great ideas, but the individual may still not make an excellent leader. Goleman (1998) also stated leaders, whether in for-profit or nonprofit entities, have a high level of what has come to be regarded as EI.

Stevens (2010) reported a research study of 515 managers at executive levels indicated managers with high EI level were more likely to excel than managers with more relevant experiences. Similarly, in a study conducted at AT&T, revealed managers with high EI were 20 times more productive than those with low EI (Bradberry & Greaves, 2009). The global study result conducted on 358 executives at Johnson & Johnson showed a relationship exist between specific skills of high performers and low or average performers (Stevens, 2010). According to Stevens (2010), high performing managers had a high level of EI than average performing one. Cherniss (2010) affirms high EI officials might improve organizational productivity more than low EI's executives.

Goleman (1998) stated EI is a necessary and crucial aspect of the management process of an organization. According to Trautmann et al.(2007), high scores in EI is associated with high performance in the workplace and life and strong skills to learn through emotions and relationships are seen as indispensable for leaders. Ross (2012) posited the capacity to self-organize across a diversity of mental conditions towards the high degree of success around the world is fundamental to today's leader.

According to Ross (2012), "Evidence suggests that leadership in the emergent world will need to be highly adaptable and creative" (p.19). Ross (2012) added leaders should be able to cope with ambiguity across cultural, political, economic and philosophical boundaries. Based on Ross (2012) EI competencies such self-consciousness, self-discipline, and public skills may be crucial in meeting the leadership needs of the emerging world (Goleman, 2004; Goleman et al., 2013). The importance of exploring the EI knowledge and its value on leadership strategies in nonprofit industries may be crucial to leadership success in this sector.

The concept of EI was defined in various ways by different scholars. Trautmann et al. (2007) stated although EI is defined in a variety of ways, the essence of the concept remained the emphasis of the researchers. The two traditional designs of EI that includes the ability-based model and the mixed model were discussed, but all emphasized the need for a leader to understand himself or herself.

The Big Five Personality Theory

The theory of personality is another critical theory that added to the framework of theories or concepts of this study. Although EI is not synonymous with personality, Mayer Salovey and Caruso (2002) maintained EI is not equivalent to possessing agreeable character traits, but EI and personality enhance each other. According to Saxena (2014), personality traits is any mental attributes that enable a person's thinking and behaving in a distinctive and enduring patterns.

In 1963, a neuropsychologist, W.I. Norman grouped personality traits into five components tagged the Five Factors Model (FFM) or the Big Five personality traits (Derue, Nahrgang, Wellman, & Humphrey, 2011; MentalHelp.net, 2016; Saxena, 2014). Among the FFM components are extraversion, agreeableness, conscientiousness, neuroticism and openness to experience (Judge & Bono, 2000; MentalHelp.net, 2016; Saxena, 2014). Over the years, the big FFM has become prominent in the psychological world and has been studies in relation to job performance, job satisfaction, performance motivations, career success in addition to organizational outcomes and other related personality domain (Saxena, 2014). The five big five components are discussed below.

Neuroticism or emotional instability. Neuroticism is a personality factor that communicates a person's possibility to be emotional, defensive, or anxious (MentalHelp.net, 2016: Saxena, 2014). According to Saxena (2014), a person that is neurotic are mostly vulnerable, self-conscious, moody, angry, and lacks self-confidence. An individual who is high in this personality traits tends to focus on negatives and can exhibit a pessimistic posture to life. According to MentalHelp.net

(2016), the neurotics tends to be reactive emotionally, and can flare-up on any inconsequential matter that naturally will not move other people.

Individuals who are low in this traits are often stable emotionally, they are calm, and are self-regulated (Judge & Bono, 2000; MentalHelp.net, 2016; Saxena, 2014). Practically, placing a neurotic in the leadership position in this volatile leadership environment of the 21st century is tantamount to keeping flammables near the fire (Hickman, 2010). According to Judge and Bono (2000), the FFM offered a platform for comprehending and differentiating a charismatic from a transformational leader.

Extraversion. Extraversion is a personality trait that highlights the social-assertiveness, activeness, boldness, energetic, and adventurousness of an individual (Saxena, 2014). According to MentalHelp.net (2016), the extroverts are often action-oriented and mostly experience positive emotions. People with this character traits are often outgoing and ready to mingle. They are mostly the people that will talk first in the group setting (MentalHelp.net, 2016). Saxena (2014) also stated that unlike the introverts, the extroverts are high in positive affectivity. MentalHelp.net (2016) said although the introvert's personality should not be mistaken for shyness, the exuberance and energy levels of the extroverts lacked in the introverts. Ployhart, Lim, and Chan (2001) stated there was a relationship between leadership, extroversion and openness. But the size of the relationships was not notable. Ployhart et al. (2001) suggested transformational leaders may possess some aspect of FFM traits.

Openness to experience. Openness to experience personality traits is reflective in the divergence of thinking, creativity,

imaginative, autonomy, and unconventionality of an individual (Judge & Bono, 2000; MentalHelp.net, 2016; Saxena,
2014). According to MentalHelp.net (2016), people who are
open to experience are sensitive to beauty, artistic oriented,
and intellectually curious. MentalHelp.net agreed with Saxena (2014) on autonomy by stating that open people tend to
be nonconforming and individualistic. People who are low in
these traits are not multitasking, narrow-minded, and suspi-
cious. Despite the limitations of the closed people, studies revealed that close thinking is correlated to great policy related
jobs and marketing (MentalHelp.net, 2016).

Agreeableness. Agreeable traits pertain to individuals who
are cooperative, trusting, generous and warm (Judge & Bono,
2000; MentalHelp.net, 2016; Saxena, 2014). According to
Saxena (2014), agreeable people are often tender-minded,
modest, straightforward, and getting along with people. One
critical feature of agreeable people is their willingness to
compromise their interests and comply with others for harmony (MentalHelp.net, 2016). But Saxena (2014) lamented
that the compromise and submissiveness may be counterproductive. But Judge and Bono (2000) posited the strongest in-
dicator of transformational leadership is agreeable.

Conscientiousness. Conscientious people are success-oriented, deliberate, diligence, responsible, and dependable
(Judge & Bono, 2000; MentalHelp.net, 2016; Saxena, 2014).
Saxena (2016) noted conscientious people tended to be reliable, goal-focus, disciplined and self-regulated. Obviously,
conscientious people are reliable and dependable fit for the
policy-making position, but the weakness of this traits is that
over-conscientious people are often workaholic, obsessive
perfectionist. According to MentalHelp.net (2016), out of the

five components of the FFM personality traits, conscientiousness and agreeableness increase as one advance in age, the
other three decreases as one advance in age. A conscientious
leader has been equated to an EI leader because of their good
sense of judge and sense of responsibility (Judge & Bono,
2000). The second heading of the literature review will be
used to discuss leadership and other leadership-related topics.

Leadership

The idea of leadership and what constitutes a good leader
sparked many arguments. Over the last 50 years, as many as
65 codification processes have been developed to discover
what embodies leadership (Neera et al., 2010). Neera et
al.(2010) reported Amazon makes available for sale more
than "60,000" variety of publications focusing on the characteristics of a leader and almost "80,000" focusing on leadership traits. The above statistics represents a 25% growth in a
decade (p. 20).

Similarly, Google quotes a large number of citations in the
concept of leaders and leadership (Neera et al., 2010). The
numerous publications on leadership are indications of the
endless quest for leadership knowledge. These publications
may be indicative of why scholars are yet to agree on a universal definition of leadership or what leadership models to
imitate (Allio, 2013). In the absence of a definitive definition
of leadership, Northhouse (2015) stated there are numerous
general characteristics that are paramount to leadership settings. These are: (a) leadership is a process, (b) leadership involve authority, (c) leadership involve objective achievement,
and (d) leadership subsists at all circumstances.

Based on the lack of an acceptable definition of leadership.

It was wise for leaders to apply EI skills such as self-awareness, social awareness, and relationship management to function on any side of the continuum in leadership performance. Since no one yardstick defines leadership, the psychological maturity of a person brought out the leader in him or her when occasion demands (Ross, 2012). EI concept may play a part continually in this direction.

Historical Overview of Leadership

Historically, leadership is one of the world's oldest preoccupations. The concept leadership is equally as old as the idea of civilization (Neera et al., 2010, p. 21; Wren, 2013). According to Allio (2013), the narratives of leadership forms the heart of human enlightenment. Leaders like "prophets, priests, chiefs, and kings" stands as emblems, archetypal, and replicas for the community in the "Old and New Testaments" (Neera et al., 2010, p. 21). The Confucius said leaders had to set honorable precedents.

The Chinese classics mentioned duties of leaders to the people (Neera et al., 2010; Wren, 2013). Safferstone (2005) added another interesting perspective to the history of leadership. According to Safferstone (2005), before the era of the Industrial Revolution a significance knowledge of how to lead an organization was drawn from the Old Testament Book of Exodus. According to Safferstone (2005), "Jethro" the father-in-law of Moses, counsels Moses about delegation of authority, selection and training of workers, and other organizational management strategies (p.959). The gleaning of leadership experience from the Bible confirms the oldness of leadership.

Studies points to the fact that leadership in the ancient

times rooted in autocracy and accomplishment of the task (Saffferstone, 2005). According to Safferstone (2005), the focus of Taylor's Scientific Management, Fayol's Administrative Management, and Gilbreth's Time and Motion study was primarily on worker efficiency. The better workers' condition of service was not the priority of these ancient leadership theorists. Wren (2013) stated the autocratic leadership style popularly adopted during the ancient times is no more popular in the 21st-century. According to Wren (2013), workforce of the 21st century, do not support autocratic leadership approach. The reason was not far fetch, 21st-century workforce are more exposed and welcome shared leadership, unlike the workforce of the previous centuries who supported being led and directed.

Wren (2013) reported during the Renaissance period; Machiavelli was of the opinion that leaders needed stability, firmness, and how to hold onto power and authority in government. Machiavelli contended where it is difficult to secure authority and power through the support of the people, craft, deceit, threat, double-dealing, and brutality should be applied. According to Wren (2013), three declarative statements was attributed to the Biblical Pharaoh. They are, "Authoritative" pronouncement comes from your mouth, your heart represent understanding, and your speech is the "shrine" of equity (p. 50).

The advent of industrialization witnessed the domination of leadership by "the Great Man theory" (Allio, 2013, p.8). The proponent of the theory (Thomas Carlyle) contended that the narrative of accomplished men is the story of great men (Allio, 2013). Within the period, leadership traits were seen as the only ingredient for success in leadership. Max Weber, a sociologist, championed the idea of charismatic leadership (Allio, 2013). According to Allio (2013), Weber stated the authority of supervisors to lead team members, can emanate from offices occupied, from proficiencies, or from enchantments. The ability of a leader to charm the follower may indicate the trust and loyalty the leader gained from his subjects and may help in effective leadership.

Leadership Theories

For the purpose of the current study, leadership models and leadership theories was used interchangeably. Wren (2013) stated the systematic study of leadership grouped into three phases. Namely, trait phase "1910 to World War-II," behavioral phase, World-11-to late "1960s" and the contingency phase, late "1960s" to the present (p. 83). Hamlin (2005) went a step further to state that leadership models could be divided into four distinct categories: (a) trait, (b) situational, (c), contingency, and (d) modern leadership, comprising of transactional and transformational leadership.

The Trait/Great Man Theories. Trait theory based on identifying characteristics that made people efficient leaders. These include factors such as personality, height, class, and age. The concept of trait theory lies on the notion that there are certain standards (appropriate trait/s) that identifies a leader from a non-leader (Faurgier & Woolnough, 2002). According to Neera et al. (2010), great man theories were based on the study of people who were already great. The primary assumption was that leaders are born and not made. The leading proponent of trait model is the Scottish historian Thomas Carlyle during the industrial revolution (Allio, 2010).

Situational Leadership Model. Situational leadership is a dynamic leadership style where the leader adopts any style according situation. According to Faugier and Woolnough (2002), the most efficient leader does not hold onto one leadership style all the time; instead, change between leadership styles as a different situation may demand different leadership options. Effective leaders adopt different leadership style depending on the proficiency of the companions. For a leader to be efficient, such must identify where the workers are in the advancement spectrum and adopt a leadership style accordingly.

Contingency Leadership Theories. Allio (2013) stated contingency leadership theorists advocated success of a leader depended on the interrelationship of some factors. Namely, (a) work needed performance, (b) the leaders and followers' relationship or connection, and (c) the positional power of the leader. Other factors include the cooperation of the members to work and the ability of the leader to exercise the authority bestowed on him or her (Allio, 2013).

Fielder contingency model in Amiri et al. (2010) indicated that the efficiency of a group is contingent on leadership style and conducts instead of traits. Contingency model depend on reciprocal faith between a leader and the worker, the clarity of duties needed performance, and the level of the authority charged to the leader. Contingency theorists argue that the leadership demands a person to use a style of conduct that synchronizes the environmental [cultural] and institutional setting (Hamlin, 2005).

Comparative Overview of Situational and Contingency Theories

There was need to explore the similarities and differences

between these two leadership models. According to Otaroghene (2012), while studying the differences between situational and contingency models highlighted the fact that some management students and even some scholars mixed up the two models as one. Exploring the similarities and differences of these leadership models clarified some misconceptions and assist organizational leaders to know which model to adopt under different situation.

Otaroghene (2012) stated situational and contingency leadership theories are similar because both emphasizes on situations. But both traded opposite path in terms of the different expectations from leaders. Theorists of the two models also highlighted there is no one right or best approach to lead an organization successfully. Otareghene (2012) emphasized "a successful leader in a given situation may become a failure in the same position in the same organization when factors around the job change" (p. 13). The changing conditions requires the management to study the organizational atmosphere (employees' behaviors) to decipher the appropriate leadership style that will contend the prevailing atmosphere (Amiri et al., 2010).

The following are the basic differences as highlighted by Otareghene (2012): Situational theorists proposed leadership style is adjustable enough for a leader to move back and forth to manage different situations. Situational leadership perspectives foresaw the possibility of a task-oriented leader adjusting to people-oriented leadership base on changing leadership needs. Contingency leadership theory based on the assumption that leadership styles are relatively inflexible or somewhat rigid. Contingency theorists contended the strict leadership style may not be instantly changed according to situations. These theorists posited management of organizations needed to take a pragmatic step to position appropriate leader to attain to the appropriate situation.

Modern Leadership Models

Although the categorization of modern leadership may not signify that these models were not in existence before now, it merely indicates the two major models that dominate the modern leadership environment. Bottomley et al. (2014) reported transactional model has been existence since the scientific management era of Fredrick Taylor. Transformational leadership came to modify the rigidity or task-oriented foundation of the transactional model.

Transactional Leadership. According to Hamlin (2005), modern leadership models is divided into transformational and transactional leadership. Hickman (2010) defined "transactional leadership" as leadership that transpires when the supervisor recompenses or punishes the follower, according to the follower's performance (p. 79). Transactional or exchange theories of leadership emphasize the relationship between a leader and a follower based on mutual exchange, signifying that nothing goes for nothing (Mahdinezhad, Suandi, Silong & Omar, 2012).

Bottomley et al.2014 noted transactional style of leadership is usually autocratic, and task oriented. Transactional leaders managed by exception, i.e., changes in management style cannot be expected unless there is a problem if it's not broken, do not fix. Transactional leaders only react when a problem occurs and tend to use negative feedback and punitive measures to staff (Amiri et al., 2010; Faugier & Woolnough, 2002). According to Sha and Said (2014), transactional style of leadership is less efficient in the management of organizational performance.

Transformational Leadership. Transformational leadership in particular is an extension of transactional leadership (Bottomley et al., 2014), but transformational leaders inspire followers to perform above what was planned and beyond what could be imagined (Mahdinezhad et al., 2013). With the application of motivational and encouragements tools, transformational leaders mostly have committed and satisfied followers. Unlike transactional leaders, transformational leaders empower followers and attend to the personal development of members (Hickman, 2010). Because of the predominant used of volunteers in NPOs, there is no doubt that NPOs leaders need to be transformative.

According to Faugier and Woolnough (2002), the ability to communicate a corporate mission of the organization, is a crucial feature of transformational leadership. Faugier and Woolnough (2002) cited Bass and Avolio as enumerating salient features of transformational leadership which included:

1) Charisma: supporters highly esteem charismatic leaders. Transformational leaders set high benchmarks and stimulate others to go the extra mile.
2) Inspirational Motivation: Transformational leaders communicate and share the innovation with the team that attracts the emotions and standards.
3) Intellectual Stimulation: Transformational leaders make work mentally invigorating for others. These leaders encourage others to question the routine and think about what they are doing and why.
4) Individualized Consideration: The peculiarity of each

employee noted and appreciated, and tasks are assigned based on potential and demands using the appropriate method.

The next section is a figure illustrating the leadership theories and models as it relates to the study.

Figure 1. Summary of Selected Models is an original design extracted from the literature review of the present research using the Microsoft Word Art of (2013).

The figure above is a descriptive presentation of the five major leadership models. The peculiarity of each model made their explanation imperative. The trait model is the oldest of the models based on identified characteristics that made a person an effective leader. The situational leadership style based on the notion that a leader can operate in any leadership situation they found themselves. The contingent model advocates the assignment of appropriate leader to lead in an appropriate leadership situation. The transformational leadership model advocates the motivation, inspiring, and encouraging the follower to perform beyond his or her usual performance level without the use of threats or compulsion. The transactional model theorists advocate the reward and punishment of the followers based on performance levels (Amiri et al., 2002; Faurgier & Woodnough, 2002; Hickman, 2010; Wren, 2013).

Other Leadership Dimensions

There are other leadership perspectives that are worth discussing in the current research study; these include servant leadership and passive- avoidance (laissez-faire leadership). The categorization of the leadership attitudes stems from the lack of a definite classification of the leadership styles. At the same time, an aspect of these leadership styles cut across the modern leadership models (transactional/ transformational leadership) enumerated above. Although the purpose of the study was not to discuss all the known leadership theories or models, the discussion of servant leadership and passive avoidance leadership style was crucial for the present study.

Servant Leadership. One leadership style that has gained appreciation by businesses and organizations in 21st century is servant leadership (Goh & Low, 2014). The conceptualization of servant leadership in recent time came to limelight through a life-long learner and an influential organizational consultant Robert. K. Greenleaf (1904-1990), (Goh & Low, 2014). According to Goh and Low (2014), Greenleaf initiated servant leadership in an essay titled "The Servant Leader" (p.17). Greenleaf maintained an essential quality of a successful leader was servant-hood. According Goh and Low (2014), servant leadership brings out attribute of trust in followers, thus making them take responsibilities when there are job-related emergencies. The caring relationship of a servant leader earns him or her confidence of the members. According to Greenleaf, Servant Leadership is a leadership perspective where the leader's cardinal motive is to serve others (Goh &

Low, 2014).

Historically, servant leadership is credited to Greenleaf (1970) described as the father of servant leadership in modern time (Parris & Peachy, 2013). Despite the attribution of servant leadership to Greenleaf (1970-1977), the original conception of servant leadership can be traced back to some great thinkers (Parris & Peachey, 2013). Parris and Peachey (2013) stated great thinkers like "Mother Theresa," "Moses," "Tubman," and "Ghandi" reflected servant leadership in their messages (p. 379). Parris and Peachy (2013) highlighted other pioneer servant leaders such as "Martin Luther King," and "Confucius" (p.379). The teachings of Jesus Christ to His disciples modeled the ultimate example of servant leadership by a number of scholars (Parris & Peachey, 2014).

Sendjaya (2015), stated although the "conceptualization" of servant leadership by Greenleaf is appealing and refreshing, the idea of servant leadership was not first introduced by Greenleaf. It was the founder of Christianity "Jesus Christ" who first incubated the concept and taught servant leadership in the Bible (p.57). Sendjaya (2015) maintained Jesus set the pace for servant leadership in His teachings in the Gospel of Mark. Jesus said "who want to become great among you must be your servant" (NIV Bible, Mark 10: 43), (Sendjaya, 2015). Jesus also demonstrated servant leadership by washing the feet of His disciplines (John, 13:13-15), (p. 59).

The significance of servant leadership to faith-based and even non-faith-based NPOs cannot be over-stressed. Because of the mission focus of NPOs, servant leadership may be the ideal leadership to meet the need of these organizations. In the opinion of Sendjaya (2015), the multidimensional nature of servant leadership includes the spiritual and ethical dimensions that made it an all-embracing construct than other leadership models. An important aspect of the construct of servant leadership is its focus on humility, authenticity, and warm reception of followers. There is a thin line between a transformational leader and a servant leader. Although, the bottom line of a transformational leader is organizational growth, the bottom line of a servant leader is the growth of the followers. These identified differences, made servant leadership more humane and positively correlated with the nonprofit group whose passion are on human development (Meyer & Taylor, 2013).

Passive Avoidance Leadership. Passive-Avoidance or Laissez-faire is a leadership style like autocratic and democratic leadership styles (Wren, 2013). Unlike other leadership styles where the leader takes the lead in showing the followers what to do, laissez-faire leadership style, explicitly avoids making decisions (Zopiatis & Constanti, 2010). In passive avoidance leadership style, the leader transfer the decision-making power about the jobs to the followers (Kurland & Hert-Lazarowitz, 2010).

One major feature of passive avoidance leadership is that leaders manage by exception. Managing by exception implies that the leaders watch the employees vigilantly to ensure no derailment from the organizational policies (Zopiatis & Constanti, 2010). Management by exception feature of passive avoidance leadership is noted by a parlance "if not broken don't fix" (Amiri et al., 2010). Management by exception feature of passive avoidance leadership made the leader be more of a reactive than the proactive leader. Leadership scholars noted that passive avoidance style of leadership do not contribute positively to the performance of the organization

(Frooman, Mendelson, & Murphy, 2012). The contribution of passive avoidance style to the present study was the independence it accorded the followers to develop thus relieving NPO leaders from excessive stress. But Zopiatis and Constanti (2010) lamented that passive-avoidance style is associated with low self-achievement or personal fulfillment and can result in the risk of stress and burnout for leaders. Kurland et al. (2010) also noted neither the autocratic or suppressive nature of transactional leadership style nor the indifference approach of the passive avoidance or laissez-faire leadership style is good for companies and the workforce. The shortcomings of the passive avoidance and transactional leadership styles paved way for the dominance of transformational and servant leadership in the 21st-century organizations.

Leadership Challenges

Leadership in the ancient days and particularly in the 21st century was/are rocked by challenges and problems (Ross, 2011). Leaders everywhere are confronted with unplanned challenges. Despite the challenges, leaders are required to act swiftly, resolutely and respectably, under the stress of increasing public suspicion (Trautman et al., 2007). According to McMurray et al. (2010), selecting a marketing orientation to meet global distribution demands is a major challenge that for-profit companies are facing.

Trautman et al. (2007) stated even the nonprofit sector not protected from the continuous changes that are battering the world. McMurray et al. (2010) reported non-profit institutions are dealing with the problem of controlling the sensitive footing between efficiency, effectiveness, goal and passion.

The successful leadership in non-profit institutions, especially faith-based, is hampered by the spiritualization of workers, chastening matters, intolerable workers conduct and intolerable workers performance.

Burnout. Burnout is another grave challenge facing leaders, especially, leaders in the faith-based non-profit organizations. Unclear or overly demanding work and lack of recognition that characterized non-profit institutions seem to stand out as the major reasons for burnout of NPO leaders (Buys & Rothmann, 2010). According to Buys and Rothmann (2010), "Burnout, is conceptualized as a physiological syndrome in response to chronic interpersonal stressors on the job. Overwhelming exhaustion and feeling of mental distance are key burnouts factors" (p. 10). Another important aspect of NPOs leader's burnout is depersonalization. According to Buys and Rothmann (2010), depersonalization connoted a disinterested and demeaned thought of someone, typified by heartless, cynical, and detached behaviors. These behaviors may be detrimental to the successful leadership of NPOs.

Training challenges. One of the challenges of the non-profit organization is the lack of a concerted effort toward training and retraining of directors and other personnel (Schoenhaus, 2002). Leadership development continues to be crucial to all organizations, especially for NPOs where the sector is witnessing the astronomical expansion in the U.S. between 1977 and 2001. Between 1977 and 2001, the employment growth rate for NPOs was (2.8%) nationally (Trautmann et al., 2007). Trautmann et al. (2007) added this rate was remarkably higher than for-profit at (1.8%) or (1.6%) for the government.

The changing nature of today's workplaces and the recent dramatic increase in the public probe increased the NPO's grave need for leaders to improve the leadership skills and competency (Trautman et al., 2007). According to Gibelman and Gelman (2001), "A need for new, trained, and committed board members matched with the need for better staff. A study conducted in Boston, Massachusetts' 3,700 NPOs revealed a lack of management training for the staff charged with day-to-day operational duties" (p. 335). The continuous neglect of NPO leadership training may affect the successful management of NPOs. The need to embark on the present study was imperative.

Family/job conflicts. The work environment in the current millennium in the for-profit and NPOs is becoming more hostile and complicated. It becomes pertinent to understand conflicts and its part in determining employee conduct and the business result (Hickman, 2010). Leaders are also in persistent scuffling to balance responsibilities of work and family life. The challenges culminated into the extremely stressful working environment. The toxic work environment have bearing on the problem of emotional self-control. Based on this background, EI surfaced as soft tools to conquer these challenges and bring about harmony in the workforce (Krishnaveni & Deepa, 2011).

Twenty First Century Leadership Demands

A clear definition of the 21st-century leadership has been difficult to reach by scholars. In order to explain what 21st-century leadership is all about, leadership scholars define 21st leadership from the lens of its purposes. According to Hickman (2010), the goal of leadership in the 21st century is to create an enabling atmosphere where workers can flourish, grow, and cohabit in peace with one another. Another goal of the 21st-century leadership is to nurture a friendship with the environment and thereby provide sustainability for future creations.

The goal of a 21st-century leader is also to generate neighborhood of mutual care and shared responsibilities –one where everyone is important, and the well-being and self-worth are honored and supported for each person (Ross, 2012). Ross (2012) also stressed the 21st-century leadership is challenged by "globalization" excessive environmental pressure, the speedier rate of information dissemination, technological advancement, and general societal changes. (p. 2). Neera et al. (2010) added another interesting dimension to 21st-century leadership challenges. According to Neera et al.(2010), illiteracy in the 21st-century will not imply the inability to read and write, but the inability to learn, "unlearn, and relearn."(p. 21). The ability to be trained and retrained may be critical skills needed in the 21st century because it explains the leaders' ability or power to be multitasking and versatile.

Increased universal consciousness in all facets of human endeavors characterizes the 21st-century economy (Ross, 2012). According to Hickman (2010), the 21st-century environment is becoming more stressful, the population issues, global warming, etc., is making the world increasingly under pressure. Hickman (2012) also stated another issue of the 21st-century economy is the rapid spread of Information globally via the world-wide-web and cable -news media. The uncontrollable flow of organizational information is challenging. These fast dissemination of information electronically impedes the resolution of internal matters within the organization (Hickman, 2010). Based on the negative impact the stressful leadership environment may have on leaders, EI skills like self-awareness may be the antidote needed to survive the hostile atmosphere.

Krell (2013) stated the chaotic, fluidity and extreme volatile features of 21st-century organizations requires people-centered leadership with a sense of purpose in achieving business goals and objectives. Krell (2013) went on to report that the number of multinational companies doubled from 35,000 in 1990 to 80,000 in 2008. These global companies operated an average of 10 international subsidiaries. Managing the increasingly diverse, mobile, and virtual workforce is a challenge. Ross (2012) stated the ability to harmonize the pressure between the outer and internal horizons of a leader is essential to the current millennium leadership growth. In other words, the mental condition of the leader will be a major determinant in the years to come.

According to Olson, Parayitam, Pinos and Twigg (2006), in the current millennium, for the profit organizations, NPOs, and governments needs leaders who can operate in multicultural environments. Leaders who are aware of differences in personalities, and recognize the need for diversity because these skills are cogent to their competitiveness and survival of the multicultural and multiethnic environment. Ross (2012) agreed with Olson et al. (2006) in recommending interpersonal leadership for the 21st-century organizations and added, the business as usual approach to leadership will not survive future leadership demands. Ross (2012) maintained that interpersonal leadership will be the ideal leadership model for the future. Interpersonal leadership conform with the principle of cooperation between different schools across a variety of fields, leading toward more mixed and composite level of understanding among individuals, groups and organizations (Ross, 2012).

Relationship-based leadership has both internal and external variation based on the concepts of variety, collaboration, Concord and synthesis (Ross, 2012). Based on the above premise, business-as-usual style of NPOs' management, characterized by a passion for serving the society without a concerted effort to train the leaders may not work in the 21st century. Therefore, the importance of undertaking the doctoral research was insightful and offered new knowledge related to the leadership roadmap of the NPOs.

Reviewing the literature on leadership highlighted rich data relevant to this study. The historical overview of leadership pointed to the principal adoption of autocratic leadership style (Safferstone, 2005). The overview indicated in the predominant used of transactional styles of Taylor and Fayol, but the arrival of the transformational model appreciated human value and dignity (Safferstone, 2005). Many challenges made leadership difficult and the need to address these challenges in view of the volatile leadership environment, in the 21st century highlighted. This qualitative study, therefore, was aimed at exploring the NPOs leaders' experiences about the value of EI on leadership strategies. The remaining part of the literature review focused on NPOs with special attention to the leadership lapses in NPOs.

Non Profit Organizations
Multiplicity of definitions. There is no globally acceptable definition of NPOs. Different authors from different back-

grounds attempted to define NPOs based on the traditional features of these organizations. Traditionally, NPOs are defined as "Self-managing organizations, sharing no profits but existing to provide a public good" (Harmer, 2006, p. 489). Lecy, Schitz, and Swedlund (2012) stated different field of study or topic of study defines NPOs according to their fields. Lecy et al. (2012) stated the organization can be designated nonprofit (NPOs), "non-governmental organizations" (NGOs), and "civil society Organizations" (CSOs), (p.434). This organization can also designate "interest groups," "advocacy networks," third-sectors, or "social movements" and many others based on the discipline (Lecy et al., 2012, p.434). Salamon and Helmut (1997) discussed different countries of the world legally made provisions or specifics on how NPOs or third sector will be classified. Salamon and Helmut added the NPOs or tax-exempt sector in U.S. is a legal establishment incorporated with exemption right from federal income tax.

Nonprofit organizations or third sector can also be defined based on the activities or mission that the organization in the sector performs. The most general activities associated with the third sector is the furtherance of what is called public interest or public purposes, i.e. some cause related to the good of the society (Salamon & Helmut, 1997). Meyer and Taylor (2013) defined NPOs as any privately owned establishments offering beneficial assistance to the public at no cost. Meyer and Taylor (2013) stated NPOs offered essential supplies and assistance above government provisions, which are less than the essential services that the "median voters" is ready to encourage (p. 138).

Historical Overview of NPOs

The importance of presenting the historical development of the NPOs cannot be overstressed. But, the multiplicity of definitions of the sector, or the lack of universally acceptable definition of NPOs by scholars made it difficult to arrive at a unique historical dimension of the sector. Different countries classified the organization according to their provisions and expectations (Lecy et al., 2012; Salamon & Helmut, 1997).

DiMaggio, Weiss, and Clotfelter (2002) stressed the difficulty and impracticality for the sector to address queries such as how many NPOs are in existence and to what extent are they starting up or folding up. Many are troubled that even the best national records are not capable of keeping accurate statistics of NPOs in existence. A seasoned nonprofit researcher maintained conducting a fact-finding study in the NPOs demands adequate experience of search engines, euphemisms, and customs that are mostly inaccessible to neophytes (DiMaggio et al., 2002). For the purpose of this dissertation, emphasis was on the history of NPOs in the United States of America.

The nonprofit or third sector is an important choice for the Americans as it encompasses a minimum of 1.6 million formal organizations and surpasses the number of informal, start-up groups or businesses. The sector incorporated some 1.2 million public-purpose establishments in areas such as health, social services, religion, environments and many others (Salamon, 1999). Meyer and Taylor (2013) stated the number of NPOs filed with the internal revenue service (IRS), grew between "1.1 million in 1995 to 1.4 million in 2005." (p. 141). The stated statistics represented an increase of "27.03%," (Meyer & Taylor, p .141). The presence of

NPOs was appreciated and valued in the provision of basic human and social services to the U.S residents more than the option of the expansive government. As a result, the sector receives more supports from the end of American Civil War in the 1860s until the launching of the New Deal in the early 1930s (Salamon, 1999).

Historically, nonprofit are relatively new institutional form. According to Lindenberg (2001) and Salamon and Helmut (1997), the notion of a nonprofit sector can be traced little more than two decades. Based on the calculation, and the reporting date by Salamon and Helmut, 90% of the third sector entities now in existence might have been formed after World War II. Yale University is reported to be the pioneer researcher on nonprofit groups in 1977 (Sims-Vanzant, 2007). During the 80s, political forces pertaining to a budget cut and policy change, pushed more social obligations to nonprofits. The budget cut and policy development compelled nonprofits in U.S to adopt for-profit business strategies, but the result was negative (Salamon, 1999).

The negative effect stems from the fact that the motive of a non-profit is different from the motive of the for-profit organization (Cheverton, 2010). To this end, there was a need to study the leadership lapses in NPOs. An in-depth study of NPO leaders' knowledge about the value of EI on leadership strategies revealed how their leadership strategies can be enhanced. Knowledge of the contribution of EI to leadership strategies in the sector can go a long way in preparing NPO leaders for the emerging dynamic leadership of the current the 21st century.

Leadership Lapses in Nonprofit Organizations

There are numbers of issues affecting nonprofit industries, but for the purpose of the present study, emphasis was on the leadership dilemmas of the NPOs. NPOs differs in dimension and scale. NPOs spanned from community and neighborhood organization with no properties and workers through billion dollar infrastructures, universities, religious centers, and health care complexes with a huge number of workers (Salamon, 1999). The challenge of leading magnificent edifices such as universities and hospitals with thousands of employees in the 21st-century calls for a properly trained leader. According to Bunchapattanasakda, Wiriyakosol, and Ya-anan (2012), leadership contributed a substantial quota in the performance of nonprofit organizations.

The fact remains that leadership in NPOs is still an illusion. According to Cheverton (2007), the nonprofit sector is still wrestling today with finding meaning and creating a standard for itself, much more its performance and leadership. Cheverton (2007) stated there is insignificant proof about the magnitude of leadership contribution to the organizational progress of NPOs. Nonprofit organizational performance is not comparable to their counterpart in for-profit organizations. But, Kramer and Nayak (2012) maintained that the strategic priority of NPOs in the 21st century should be leadership development.

One of the dilemmas of the nonprofits or third sectors' effective leadership is the "spiritualization" of employee discipline issues (McMurray et al., 2010, p. 436). The entanglement of employee discipline with spirituality or morality made it difficult for a leader to enforce discipline and achieve optimum performance. Unlike the for-profit organizations that are driven by profit motive, NPOs are mission-driven (Cheverton, 2007). The passion for providing selfless services to the society is the hallmark of the NPOs. Driven by a passion for serving without a corresponding effective management plans, may be detrimental to the organizational survival. Cheverton (2007) maintained an intense dedication to mission or passion can also stifle innovation, resulting in some nonprofits or third sector's functioning below optimum performance.

Changing leadership focus in the 21st century and ongoing attraction to adopt the for-profit management strategies (Lindenberg, 2001), propelled some NPOs to consider the for-profit management strategies (Bunchapattanasakda et al., 2012). The adoption may go a long way in revitalizing the dwindling management of the NPOs. But, a critical look at the adoption idea, reveals that there may be a problem in the long run. The fundamental reason is NPO and for-profit are different organizations with different motives.

Nonprofit organizations are mission-driven while for-profit organizations are profit-driven (Bunchapattanasakda et al., 2012; McMurray et al., 2010). What is needed, may be a context-based leadership training that takes into consideration the peculiar nature of the NPOs (McMurray et al., 2010). The new framework may serve the purpose better than adopting a strategy that is not germane to NPOs. Based on these controversies, the need to understand the EI perceptions of NPO leaders about the value of EI no leadership strategies was crucial.

Methodologies Used by Other Researchers with Related Topics

There are a plethora of studies conducted within the topic

of EI and leadership by researchers across sectors; this may be attributable to the broad claim that EI cannot be done without by leaders (Goleman, 2002). Although there are disagreements here and there among scholars about the role of EI on leadership, Khalili (2013) for instance stated to ascertain the relationship between EI and leadership strategies, additional studies are needed. Researchers like Michel, Stegmaier, and Sonntag (2010), reported organization's failure to improve stakeholder's investments, sustainable growth and earnings are as a result of the failure to fully understand the construct of EI. Adeoye and Torubelli (2011) stated organizational commitment is measured by the leaders' knowledge of EI. Researchers such as Lopez-Zafra et al. (2012), reported that the ability of a leader to make effective decisions and commitment to the organization is determined by the leader's EI awareness and conscientiousness.

Literature so far reviewed indicated that plethora of EI research was conducted using the quantitative method. At the same time, a couple of EI studies were also done as qualitative research. Only a handful of EI studies were done using mixed methods. The construct of EI has also been examined in various conceptual areas using different designs. The commonest research designs discovered is quantitative correlational design. Jimenez (2016) conducted a correlational study of 180 nonprofit managers in Texas. Jimenez's study result showed a positive correlation between EI and transformational leadership style, but no relationship was found between EI and transactional leadership. Goleman (1998) conducted a similar study with approximately 200 leaders of the major global companies, and the result revealed EI at the top-level of an organization is the sine qua non to leadership. Goleman

(2004) carried out a correlational research of 188 leaders in the major global companies. Goleman's study result revealed while technical skills such as long-term vision and big picture thinking were performance indicators, EI was found to be twice essential for job performance at all levels than technical expertise.

According to Garcia (2015), a correlational researcher explores the extent of the relationship between variables (dependent and independent). Garcia's (2015) correlational study of 77 faculties and 351 students which explore relationship between leadership styles, conflict management, and EI skills of participants and quality of education found a positive correlation among the variables. In a controlled setting, the use of quantitative descriptive designs examines the existence of a relationship among variables (Creswell, 2013; Garcia, 2015; Leedy & Ormrod, 2010). Empirical models also used the controlled environment to manipulate both the dependent variables and independent variables to determine the relationship (Creswell, 2013; Leedy & Ormrod, 2010).

Qualitative research methodology using various designs was found to be widely employed in EI and leadership research. Qualitative researchers applied the non-numerical approach in the investigations of the phenomenon of human interest (Creswell, 2013; Leedy & Ormrod, 2010). Various EI and leadership research are explored from the perspectives of the lived experiences, case studies, narrative or story-telling inquiries, interpretative studies, exploratory studies, descriptive investigations, and many others. A phenomenological study of 24 frontline healthcare workers conducted by Snodgrass (2015) found servant leadership positively affected employees' environments and engagement. The smooth application of the qualitative method in the study under review in exploring the participants' lived experiences suggests the use of the similar method in the present study (Leedy & Ormrod, 2010; Snodgrass, 2015).

Keung and Rockinson-Szapkiw (2013) also conducted a multivariate correlational case study of 193 international school leaders in 190 different countries and found a positive correlation between cultural intelligence and transformational leadership. Cultural intelligence conceptualized from four multidimensional constructs of behavioral, cognitive, metacognitive, and motivational divisions of cultural intelligence, refers to the ability of an individual to operate efficiently and lead in a diversely cultural environment (Keung & Rockinson-Szapkiw, 2013). The researcher adopted the Cultural Intelligence Scale and the Multifactor Leadership Questionnaire 5X instruments with basic multiple regression analysis to arrive at the results. The researcher concluded that cognitive and behavioral cultural intelligence were best predictors of transformational leadership and recommended cultural intelligence training for multicultural leadership (Keung & Rockinson-Szapkiw, 2013).

Another methodology adopted in EI research is mixed methods. Mixed methods are unique in the sense that it synthesized both quantitative and qualitative methods together in an investigative setting. According to Onwuegbuzie and Collins (2010), Teddlie and Tashakkori define mixed methods as "research in which the researcher gathers and examines data, combines the findings, and draw inferences using both qualitative and quantitative methods in a single study" (p.15). The mixed methods' study of Estelle, Beth, and Lynn (2013) using pre/post-test design revealed an inconclusive result because of the unexpected low emotional response among the participants. This pilot study explored the quantitative and qualitative strands of the study sequentially before arriving at the conclusions. According to Leedy and Ormrod (2010), one of the unique features of mixed methods over other methods is a triangulation of data. Data triangulation enables a researcher to conduct a cross process verifications resulting in a more reliable result (Creswell, 2013).

In another mixed methods research using pre-post EQ-i assessment and semi-structured interviews, Dolev and Leshem (2016) conducted a pilot study of 21 teachers in Israel. The study result found that participants perceived that EI training enhances their EI skills based on Bar-On EI model. According to Dolev and Leshem (2016), the combined use of structured interview findings and EQ-i scores triangulate the study results and also enlarges the scope of the research. Unlike quantitative and qualitative researchers who relied on the single source of data to determine the research result, mixed methods researchers combine data sources for positive findings (Creswell, 2013; Leedy & Ormrod, 2010; Merriam, 2016).

Chapter Summary

Leadership was found to be the world oldest preoccupation and leadership concept was also found to be as old as the notion of civilization. Amazon has almost 60,000 varieties of books on the leaders and over 80,000 on leadership for sale. Sub-elements such as the historical overview of leadership, leadership models, the leadership challenge, and the 21st-century leadership were reviewed in this literature review section. The previous emphasis on technically intelligent leaders gave way to emotionally intelligent leadership in the 21st century.

Another literature category was in nonprofit organizations. Nonprofit organizations are equally a crucial aspect of the current study. The lack of the universally accepted definition of nonprofit among authors inhibited accurate historical overview of nonprofit with a universal outlook. Different countries in the world made provision and specifics on which organization should be classified as nonprofit. Most authors of nonprofits rely on the general characteristics of a nonprofit in defining the term. The delivery of public services or public functions was identified as the salient feature of nonprofits. Also reviewed in this section were the related methodologies and designs adopted by other researchers. The next section, Chapter 3 will be used to explain the methodologies of the study.

Chapter 3
Methodology

■ The qualitative descriptive inquiry is a descriptive study that engages shared experiences of the phenomena. The method enables the researcher to understand the experiences of the participants and also develop a deeper understanding of the phenomenon (Creswell, 2015).

The purpose of this qualitative descriptive study was to explore and examine the perceptions of the NPO leaders about the value of EI on leadership strategies in the City of Richmond, Virginia. In Chapter 1, the study problem statement, the background of the research, and the significance of the study were discussed. Also examined in chapter 1 were the research questions, the nature of the Study, the conceptual framework, study assumptions, limitations, and delimitations of the study. In Chapter 2, literature covering a historical overview of EI, critical review of EI, and EI models were discussed.

The literature on leadership theories, leadership challenges, 21st-century leadership, historical overview of NPOs, and the leadership lapses of NPOs were also reviewed. In Chapter 3, the research method and design selected in Chapter 1 was elaborated. The appropriateness of the design, the population, data collection process, data analysis, the study confidentiality and the informed consent of the study participants was discussed.

Research Method and Design Appropriateness

The descriptive purposes of the study, the research problem, and the research questions contributed to the selection of qualitative research method for the present study. According to Arbnor and Bjerke (2009), in any research situation, it is imperative that the research problem determine the selection of the study method and design and not the other way round. Qualitative research offered ample explorative avenues needed in the current study. Yin (2015) stated qualitative research is designed to explore the differences of complicated human conduct in a particular setting.

Guteng (2005) defined qualitative research as a multi-method system of inquiry that employs a real-life approach to answering questions of the experiential interest. According to Leedy and Ormrod (2010), the goal of the qualitative researcher is to investigate the situation to obtain firsthand information about the issues of concern. The appropriate research design for the in-depth description of the participants' perceptions is qualitative descriptive inquiry (Thomas & Magilvy, 2009).

Quantitative research was not adequate for the present study, as the focus of the study was on the experiences of NPO leaders, offering no quantitative data for analysis (Steven, 2010). According to Onwuegbuzie and Collins (2010), quantitative study is "a study where the researcher determines what to verify, ask specific and narrow questions, collect numeric data from participants, analyze these data using statistics and conduct an inquiry in an objective manner" (p.39). Similarly, Leedy and Ormrod (2010), stated quantitative researchers answer questions about relationships between numerical variables with the purpose of explaining, predicting, and controlling phenomena.

The qualitative descriptive inquiry is a descriptive study that engages shared experiences of the phenomena. The method enables the researcher to understand the experiences of the participants and also develop a deeper understanding of the phenomenon (Creswell, 2015). The use of qualitative inquiry or in-depth interpretive process to harness the experiences of participants offered adequate result. Also, the focus of the researcher was not about making inferences or predictions. But the goal of the researcher was to investigate the perceptions of NPO leaders about the value of EI on leadership using the descriptive approach.

Mixed methods research would have served the purpose of the present research, but the existence of many research designs in mixed model was a challenge (Leech & Onwuegbuzie, 2010). According to Ivankova, Creswell, and Stick (2006), mixed methods is a process of gathering, examining, and mixing both quantitative and qualitative data at some stage of the study process for the purpose of gaining adequate comprehension of the research problem. Leedy and Ormrod (2010) stated mixed methods researchers divide attention to the quantitative and qualitative strands sequentially or concurrently. The division of attention to two methods at the same time created a challenge of providing limited attention to the area of high priority (qualitative), (Leedy & Ormrod, 2010).

The qualitative method selected for the present study was conceptualized within the framework or paradigm of constructivism. According to Guteng (2005), constructivists' belief system or worldview are of the opinion that experiences can best be understood from the perspective of those whose life reflects it. The constructivist worldview that upholds the importance of the researcher's interaction with the participants to reconstruct the experiences follows the tenet of the descriptive study (Guteng, 2005). Creswell (2009) stated using a descriptive qualitative inquiry details the participants' perception of the value of EI on their leadership.

Among the top four qualitative models namely: Grounded theory, ethnography, case study, and phenomenology, grounded theory was the second best alternative for the study. Despite the similarity of methodology, grounded theory was rejected because the primary objective of the research practitioner was not to build theory. Grounded theory is a qualitative study design that involves developing a theory based on the data collected instead of collecting data after a theory has already formed (Purpose of Research, 2015). Although the present research may lay a groundwork for theory building, the holistic, descriptive, and independence of descriptive inquiry made grounded theory design inadequate for the present research (Schwandt, 2015)

The best alternative design for this dissertation was the narrative inquiry. But the narrative inquiry was rejected because the researcher's goal was not to reduce the research to mere storytelling as practiced by narrative inquirer (Creswell, 2012). Although, the collection of stories, reporting the experiences of individuals, and chronologically ordering the meaning of those experiences could add a qualitative rigor to the study; but descriptive inquiry combined rigor, theory formation, and flexibility, and thick descriptive abilities to the study (Creswell, 2012). Creswell (2012) stated an aspect of story-telling, a great feature of narrative inquiry is already embedded in the descriptive inquiry design adopted in this dissertation.

Descriptive research was also found to be more comprehensive than other qualitative models because it describes the participants' experiences as expressed in a lived and told stories a feature of phenomenology and narrative inquiry (Creswell, 2012). Magilvy and Thomas (2009) asserted that the thick description of the participants' experiences afforded the researcher a rich platform for better comprehension of the respondents' viewpoints. Above all, the drafting of interview questions based on the hypothetical future situation could not have been properly addressed using narrative inquiry than the descriptive one. The descriptive ramifications of the adopted design were the right fit in dealing with the research question and the purpose of this study (Arbnor & Bjerke, 2009).

Purpose of Research (2015) defined descriptive inquiry as an effort to examine and explore the participants' experiences by describing the event in details and supplying the missing information for adequate comprehension. According to Purpose of Research (2015), most often, descriptive inquiry provide sufficient information about the phenomenon because of it full descriptive capacity. The application of basic qualitative inquiry assisted researchers gain understanding of how people construct meaning of their world (Merriam, 2009). Descriptive inquiry also assisted the respondents to describe their events adequately while expressing personal views about the events (Wong & Ng, 2008). Because of the lack of information about the value of EI on the leadership of NPOs, a careful description of the event may reveal more details about the participants' perceptions (Purpose of Research, 2015).

Seidman's interview phases were used in the data collection. According to Guteng (2005), Seidman's clearly examines the goal of employing three phase interviews in exploring a social phenomenon of the experiential interest. Seidman's in-depth interview process described as 'a conversation with a purpose' is a dependable data collection approach adopted by most qualitative researchers (Guteng, 2005). A cardinal merit of the qualitative descriptive study was the open-ended questions and probing. Open-ended questions and probing allows participants the opportunity to answer questions in their words, rather than to force them to choose from fixed responses, as quantitative methods (Qualitative Research Methods, 2015). The next section will be used to explore the research question of the study.

Research Questions

For the purpose of the present study, two research questions (RQ1) and (RQ 2) were examined.

RQ1: What are the perceptions of NPO leaders concerning

the value of EI on leadership strategies in Richmond Virginia? The purpose of the question was to explore the perceptions of NPO leaders about the value of EI on their leadership strategies. The answer to the research question helped in articulating the current position of NPO leaders in terms of emotional awareness and their leadership strategies (George et al., 2014). The answer to the research question also helped in bridging the knowledge gap in the current area of study. McMurray et al. (2010) maintained while there are many research studies in the for-profit sector, the nonprofit sector lags behind in the research dealing with EI and leadership strategies

Exploring the perceptions of NPO leaders about the value of EI on leadership was speculated to reveal knowledge gap that needs filling. Theodoridis (2014) stated knowledge emerged when we set aside all previous habits of thought and breaking down the mental barriers these patterns places along the horizons of our thinking. The purpose of this question was also to explore whether EI knowledge have any bearing on the leadership of NPOs. Goleman (2004) enumerated the five distinct EI skills namely: (a) self-awareness, (b) self-management, (c) relationship management, (d) social-awareness, and (e) motivation. These skills contribute individually and severally to the performance of leaders. The second research question for the study was:

RQ2: What are the perceptions of the faith-based NPO leaders compared to that of the non-faith-based NPO leaders concerning the value of EI on their leadership strategies in Richmond Virginia? The purpose of this question was to examine the differences in opinion if any about the value of EI on leadership among the two subdivisions of the NPOs. The

need to examine the differences was unconnected with the asserted over-spiritualization of the employee discipline among
the faith-based NPO leaders (McMurray et al., 2010). See
Appendix B for interview questions. The next section will be
used to discuss the conceptual framework of the study.

Population and Sample Size

The population for the present study comprised of leaders
in the faith-based and non-faith-based NPOs in the US. The
sample for the study was drawn from NPO leaders operating
in the City of Richmond, Virginia. The targeted leaders had
the basic knowledge of EI or its essential components. The
leaders were drawn from an executive position
(President/CEO/Senior Pastor/Executive Director, Manager,
Associate Pastor, or Assistant Manager), with a basic qualification of a bachelor degree and above. The selected faith-
based leaders had a minimum congregation membership of
20 and a basic leadership experience of 3 years. The non-
faith-based leaders had a basic leadership experience of 3
years and a minimum of five employees.

The decision to select Richmond stemmed from the rich
social, economic, and political heritage of the City. According
to Kenzer (2001), Richmond was in the 1850s described as a
city of political, economic and social values. Another reason
for the selection of Richmond was the proximity of the research area to the researcher that offers lower cost option
compared to other alternatives. The city of Richmond is en-
dowed with various forms of NPOs. Historical universities,
hospitals, charities, and churches such as Virginia Commonwealth University (VCU), St Mary's Hospital, Salvation
Army, Goodwill, and the Baptist church are all located in the

City of Richmond.

The study participants were 14 leaders from faith-based or non-faith-based divisions of NPOs (Mason, 2010). The study participant met the data saturation requirement of the study (Kerr, 2010; Merriam, 2009). The participant recruitment continued using the purposive sampling until the acceptable participants were enlisted. According to Marshall, Cardon, Poddar, and Fontenot (2013), data saturation connotes the continuous recruitment of participant into the study until the data set is exhausted. Data saturation was attained when enough information to replicate the study was collected and an additional theme was no longer practicable (Bernard, 2012; Creswell, 2013; Fusch & Ness, 2015; O'Reilly & Parker, 2012; Walker, 2012).

Recently, the right number of interviews to attain data saturation has raised contention among scholars. While some argued that three consecutive interviews with no new information revealed lead to saturation; some stated that five or six one-hour interviews result in saturation, some suggested 10, and some suggested 12 interviews (Creswell, 2013; Ives Tay Assoc CIPD BBA, 2014). Bernard (2014), concluded deciding the right number of interviews for data saturation is difficult; "researcher take what he can get" (Fusch & Ness, 2015, p. 1409). O'Reilly and Parker (2012) on-the-other-hand, based their definition of data saturation on the length of an interview as opposed to the number of interviews. Despite the differences of opinion about data saturation, using data saturation to determine the sample size added to the content validity of this study (Fusch & Ness, 2015; Leedy & Ormrod, 2010).

Field Test

A field test was conducted to test the validity of the study through pretesting of the interview questions. The value of a field test of interview questions was to ensure interview questions were valid and fit for the study. According to Neuman (2009), field study verify the clarity and validity of the study using a small number of study participants. The drafted interview questions were tested on three faculty member from the University of Phoenix. The three faculty members were contacted through email and the interview was done through the phone. (See, Appendix C).

Sampling Frame and Technique

The sampling frame for the present qualitative descriptive study consisted of all the NPO leaders who resided in the city of Richmond, Virginia during the time of the research. A sample size of 14 participants was recruited to take part in the study. Singleton and Straits (2009) defined sampling frame as a collection of cases from which the sample is selected. The need for qualitative rigor and the subjective nature of qualitative research made it expedient for recruitment of fewer study participants (Creswell, 2013; Leedy & Ormrod, 2010; Mason, 2010). Mason (2010) stated the sampling size for qualitative study range from five to 65 participants.

For the purpose of ensuring qualitative rigor, the participants were purposefully selected to take part in the study (Patton, 1990). The following were the step by step sampling process for the study: The primary sampling method was purposive sampling because of the huge size of Richmond population (Patton, 1990; Routio, 2007). Nonprofits section of Richmond Yellow Pages and Bureau of NPOs in Richmond was consulted for the sample.

An emails and phone calls was sent to prospective participants. The first phase of Seidman's interview process was used in the pre-interviewing of the prospective participants.

Informed Consent

Informed consent is a vital document in research involving human subjects (Leedy & Ormrod, 2010). Before data collection, the study was approved by the Institutional Review Board (IRB). The researcher also completes a web-based training for human subject research organized by Collaborative Institutional Training Initiative (CITI). In enlisting members to the study, the process was purely voluntary, i.e., the prospective members were willing to take part in the study out of free-will and could opt-out at will.

According to Neuman (2009), the relevant information that forms the informed consent were; (a) brief overview of the research purpose, (b) duties required of members, (c) benefits and risks involved, (d) voluntary participation clause, (e) participant confidentiality clause, (f) researcher contact information and complaints contact, and (g) participant and researcher signature. The primary purposes of the informed consent were the protection and safety of the participants. The researcher secured a signed consent form from each participant attesting to the voluntary ramification of participation and opt-out option any time during the study (See Appendix A). The consent form was ink-signed by all participants before the data collection.

Confidentiality

Confidentiality of the participant's information is a crucial element in any human subject research. For the purpose of the current study, confidentiality of participant's information was assured by electronically accessing all discernible information (Leedy & Ormrod, 2010). The researcher maintained and stored the respondent's private information and study data in an encrypted file. The confidentiality and privacy of the participant's data were maintained according to the IRB's regulations.

The study results were presented as an aggregate response or in a generalized format. Participants' personal data was not identified in data analysis and interpretation. Also, the used of the study findings in journals, books, presentations, conferences, or lectures will take a generalized format to protect personal information from the participants. The information gathered from the participants will be stored in secured space for a minimum of 3 years after which it will be shredded.

Geographic Location

The current qualitative descriptive study was conducted in the City of Richmond, Virginia. The purpose of the study was not to generalize the result but to explore the knowledge of the NPO leaders about the value of EI on leadership strategies. A purposive sampling process was used in the recruitment of the study participants (Patton, 1990; Routio, 2007).

Data Collection

Data collection process for this qualitative research began after the research was approved by IRB. Before the data collection, the researcher's CITI certification status was current.

Purposeful and reputational sampling technique was adopted in collecting data for the study. According to Routio (2007), there are reasons for the adoption of nonrandomized sampling. The first reason is attributed to large population size making it impossible for everybody to be interviewed.

The second reason is attributed to the impossibility of gaining access to all people in the target population. The third reason is when the objective of the study do not require the exact result. The City of Richmond is a huge City with a population of about 210,000. It was impossible to interview everybody; therefore, nonrandomized sampling was ideal for the study. Data for the current descriptive inquiry was collected based on Seidman's second and third interview phases. The first phase of Seidman's interviews was set aside for pre-screening of the participants based on the study participation criteria (Seidman, 2013).

The following were the step by step process of collecting data for the study:

Initial emails with a letter of introduction and phone calls explaining the purpose of the study was sent to prospective participants purposively (Patton, 1990), see (Appendix D). Permission to use premises was not applicable to this study. A face-to-face and in-person interviews were conducted in an arranged place. Other interviews were conducted through Skype or phone depending on the participant's preference. Participants were pre-interviewed for qualification and selected for the study (Seidman Phase One Interviews). Informed consent was acknowledged and ink-signed by selected participants before interviews (see, Appendix A).

The selected participants took part in the second phase of Seidman's interviews (Guteng, 2005; Seidman, 2013). Open-ended questions with a response-guide and conversational prompt was used for interviews (Saliu, 2013). The interview questions revolved around the research question and problem statement. The interview was recorded using an electronic voice recorder with the permission of the respondents. Any respondent who did not consent to recording was politely dropped. Interview responses was transcribed verbatim immediately after the interviews.

The participants reviewed, amended, and approved their individual transcripts (Third Phase of Seidman's Interviews). See Appendix B, for the suggested interview questions for the study.

Instrumentation

Instrumentation in a research study describes the tools or instruments that enhance the conduct of the investigation. For the purpose of the current qualitative descriptive inquiry the set of interview questions was the instrument (See, Appendix B). The semi-structured interview questions were field tested using faculty members for validation (Leedy & Ormrod, 2010). Open-ended questions and probing were used to allow the participants the opportunity to answer questions in their words, rather than to force them to choose from fixed responses, as in the quantitative methods (Qualitative Research Methods, 2015).

The field test met its primary purpose of validating the interview questions. The field test led to the rephrasing of some of the questions. Example, one of the questions was "what do you understand by the term EI?" It was rephrased to "what is EI to you." The rephrasing of the question was necessary because EI as a concept may mean different thing to different people. The rephrased question afforded participants an opportunity to answer the question anyhow they perceive. The rephrased question highlighted the open-ended feature of qualitative interview questions and preventing the yes or no answers (Saliu, 2013). The result of the field test attested to the feasibility of the questions in meeting the need of the study and pointed out where participants may have difficulties (See, Appendix C). Finally, the power of the interview questions in revealing the EI perceptions of the field test participants validated the interviews questions for the study.

Data Analysis

The selection of data analysis process in a qualitative study has been found to be difficult because of the subjective nature of qualitative studies and the varieties of research goals (Glaser & Landel, 2013). Leech and Onwuegbozie (2011) stated some types of research question/s and types of data can compound the confusion of a novice researcher in selecting analysis type. For the purpose of the current descriptive study, a computer-assisted coding system (NVivo) was used. Glaser and Landel (2013) noted the computer-assisted coding process (NVivo) is perhaps the most popular and reliable method of qualitative data analysis.

The undesirability if not impracticability of analyzing large data manually, made manual method unfit for this study (Leech & Onwuegbozie (2011). Also, the use of computer-assisted coding system (NVivo) increased the qualitative rigor of a study (Leech & Onwuegbozie, 2011). A key advantage of NVivo over manual method was its ability to analyze data from four major sources—namely, documents, talk, drawings/photographs/videos, and observations (Leech & Onwuegbozie, 2011). Even getting better, the current version of NVivo (NVivo10), analyzed data from social media such as Facebook, Twitter, LinkedIn, WhatsApp, etc., (QSR International, 2015).

The step by step data analysis process for this descriptive study was as follow.

1) Immediately after interviews, the interview scripts were transcribed verbatim using Microsoft words.
2) The individual interview script was reviewed and ratified by the participants before data analysis.
3) The primary data analysis process follows the computer-assisted coding system (NVivo10) where emerging themes were generated and auto-coded (Glaser & Landel, 2013).
4) The generated codes were repeated by the use of a computer software, NVivo10.
   The repetition of codes ensures consistency of coding (Oliver, 2004).
5) NVivo10 was used to run series of queries such as the most frequent words and a comparative overview of the faith-based and the non-faith-based leaders.

Trustworthiness

Scholars and indeed qualitative researchers maintained that precision and objectivity of the study result are not the primary focus of the qualitative researchers. Qualitative researchers used nomenclature such as transferability, confirmability, dependability, and credibility (trustworthiness), to denote the equivalencies of validity in the quantitative studies (Chowdhury, 2015; Lincoln & Guba, 1985; Merriam, 2016; Shenton, 2004). The trustworthiness of the current study was ensured under the following empirical equivalencies.

Dependability. To ensure the trustworthiness of a study, a question like "Is the study accurate or dependable?" needs to be asked and the answer needs to be positive. Qualitative dependability is equivalent to quantitative reliability (Chowdhury, 2015; Shenton, 2004). Irrespective of the documented difficulties of attaining dependability, this study's dependability was ensured through detailed note taking, adequate taping tools, accurate transcription, and data replication (Lincoln & Guba, 1985). Also, detailed method descriptions, cross-reviews by peers, auto-coding, and re-coding of data also ensured the dependability of this study (Thomas & Magilvy, 2011).

Confirmability. The trustworthiness and confirmability of a study can be guaranteed if a yes answer is gotten from the question like "Can the study be replicated?" Qualitative confirmability is synonymous with objectivity in quantitative research (Chowdhury, 2015; Shenton, 2004). For the purpose of the current descriptive research, the conformability of the study was instituted by following the qualitative research due process. According to Leedy and Ormrod (2010), the researcher's rigor is the primary instrument in qualitative research. Scrutinizing of the study process and ensuring the transparency of the research process initiates both dependability and confirmability (Creswell, 2013). According to Thomas and Magilvy (2011), confirmability of the study can be guaranteed once dependability, credibility, and transferability, of the study, are established. The researcher's critical self-evaluation and culture of detailed note taking ensured the confirmability of the current study (Magilvy, 2011).

Credibility. The trustworthiness and credibility can be assured if a positive answer is gotten from the question such "Is the study credible?" qualitative credibility is equivalent to internal validity in quantitative studies (Chowdhury, 2015; Shenton, 2004). The absence of direct triangulating data in the study made the researcher depend greatly on the personal self-reflections for credibility (Merriam, 2016). Another tool used in determining the credibility of the current study was peer cross-review, peer examination or debriefing, and member checking (Magilvy, 2011). The researcher's close relationship with doctoral colleagues provided adequate avenues for peer review. The researcher also sought for meaningful feedback from trusted participants in the process called member checking (Creswell, 2016). The most reliable approach for ascertaining the credibility of a study has been found to be member checking (Lincoln & Guba, 1985; Shenton, 2004).

Transferability. Qualitative trustworthiness and transferability can be ascertained if a yes answer is gotten from a question such as "Can the study be transferred to a larger population?" Qualitative transferability aligned with a generalization or external validity in quantitative studies (Chowdhury, 2015; Shenton, 2004). Adequate explanations of the members' responses, including the settings, field notes, and direct quotes (thick description), can enhance transferability (Lincoln & Guba, 1985; Thomas & Magilvy, 2011). For the purpose of the present study, transferability was ensured through a thick description of the participants' data, detailed field notes, and proper research setting. In a simple summation, Chowdhury (2015), maintained the reader is obligated to use the information about the study at their disposal to decide the transferability of a study to a different setting. Chowdhury

(2015) did not agree with the equation of qualitative transferability to quantitative generalization and external validity. Based on this submission, the study results will be published for the interested reader to digest and make transferability decision.

Chapter Summary

The purpose of this qualitative descriptive inquiry was to explore the perceptions of NPO leaders about the value of EI on leadership strategies in the City of Richmond, Virginia. In Chapter 3, the focus was on the elaboration of the methodology previously introduced in Chapter 1. The research method chosen for the research study was qualitative descriptive inquiry using Seidman's three phase interviews. The choice of the descriptive inquiry based on its power to explore a topic with unknown information.

The quantitative method did not meet the needs of the research because of its emphasis on statistical worldview. The present study was exploring the participants' experiences, perceptions, and knowledge offering no statistical data for analysis. Other qualitative designs could not also challenge the descriptive power of the chosen design. Studies revealed that researchers seeking to explore a phenomenon with unknown information or fewer literature rely on descriptive inquiry (Purpose of Research, 2015).

In Chapter 3, the informed consent and confidentiality of the participant's information was discussed. The informed consent document assured the participants of the voluntary nature of involvement in the study. The confidentiality document on-the-hand ensured the privacy and security of the participant's information. The geographical location of the study was the City of Richmond, Virginia. The sampling frame for this study was 14 NPO leaders located in the City of Richmond.

In Chapter 3, the researcher summarized the approval process by the quality review methods (QRM) and how it preceded the data collection stage of the study. The rigor and competence of the researcher and interview questions were highlighted as crucial instruments for the research. The qualitative credibility and dependability of the study instruments enhanced the trustworthiness of the study result. The present descriptive study did not rely on the precision and accuracy criteria of the quantitative study but based on the subjective and qualitative credibility and dependability. The next chapter (Chapter 4) will be used primarily to discuss the data collection and data analysis phases of the study.

Chapter 4
Results

■ The initial process of data classification and categorization was done through auto coding of the interview transcripts based on the interview questions. The auto coding queries were done by entering all the interview questions and participants' responses in the NVivo10. Before running the queries, the interview questions and the answers were marked for identification.

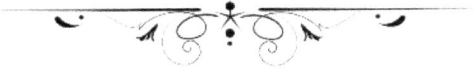

The purpose of this qualitative descriptive inquiry was to explore and examine the perceptions of NPO leaders about the value of EI on leadership strategies in the City of Richmond, Virginia. The general business problem was the lack of emotionally competent leadership in the nonprofit sector resulting in high rate of fraud and scandals among the industry leaders. The specific business problem was the perceptions of the NPO leaders about the value of EI on leadership strategies in Richmond Virginia was unknown resulting in the training program decisions dilemmas for the sector. The descriptive inquiry design was found to be suitable in the description of the data used in this study. This chapter discussed a brief description of the field study, the data collection procedure, the participants' demographics, the analysis of the interview questions and the emerging themes, and the comparative overview of the faith-based and non-faith-based NPOs. Chapter 5 addressed the conclusion, summary of the results, and recommendations.

Analysis of the Field Test

The validity and credibility of the interview questions were assured through a brief field test of the interview questions. The participants of the field test were drawn from three faculty members of the University of Phoenix. The faculty members were solicited and recruited through emails and phone calls. The interviews were done through the phones, and the response was jotted in a notebook. The primary purpose of the field test was to validate the interview questions. Seidman's second and third interview phases were used to explore the professional experiences of the participants about EI knowledge and leadership. The responses were played back to the participants for ratification.

Results of the Field Test

The field test met its primary purpose of validating the interview questions. The field test led to the rephrasing of some of the questions. Example, one of the questions was "what do you understand by the term EI?" It was rephrased to "what is EI to you." The rephrasing of the question was necessary because EI as a concept mean different thing to different people. The rephrased question afforded participants the opportunity to answer the question anyhow they perceive. The rephrased question highlighted the open-ended feature of qualitative interview questions and prevented the yes or no answers. The field test revealed the feasibility of the questions in meeting the need of the study and pointed out where participants may have difficulties (See, Appendix C). Finally, the power of the interview questions to reveal the EI knowledge of the field test participants validated the interviews questions for the study.

Data Collection Procedure

The data collection for the study followed a purposive sampling method. The actual data collection started after the IRB approval of the research. The data gathering for the study took place from February 6th –March 4th. The initial emails and phone calls explaining the purpose of the study was sent to prospective participants purposively. The researcher's professional colleagues also assisted in recommending participants to the study. Based on the estimated number of participants, a total of 45 volunteers were contacted for participation in the study. Out of the 45 volunteers, 38 were qualified for participation in the prescreening phase. Nine of the volunteers did not follow through the process.

Out of the 29 remaining qualified volunteers, 14 were selected for participation based on other qualities they possess than others. Before the selection of the 14 participants, all the

45 contacted volunteers were prescreened. The participants prescreening represented the phase one of the Seidman's interview phases and was based on the prequalification criteria (See, Appendix B). Before the real interviews (Seidman Interviews Phase Two), the 14 selected participants were required to ink-signed the informed consent form.

The interviews sessions took place in a serene environment conducive for sound mental articulation. Interviews of six of the members were done face-to-face in an arranged places of the participants' choosing. The remaining eight members were interviewed over the phone. Because of the abstract nature of some of the questions, the interviewees were supported with response guides and conversational prompts. Each response was recapitulated to verify the exact perspective of the participants. Immediately after each interviews, the response was transcribed using the Microsoft Words for analysis. The final transcripts were emailed to individual participants for verification and ratification before analysis (Seidman's Interviews Phase 3).

Participants' Demographics

The participant demographics was a crucial aspect of this research because of the qualifications needed for participation in the study. The participants in the study were evenly divided into Faith-Based Leaders (FBLs) and Non-Faith-Based Leaders (NFBLs). The participants' demographics presented in this chapter was not a detailed demographic data normally added in the appendix. The demographics were simply to highlight the qualification of the participants for the study based on the recruitment criteria. Information about the participants' gender was not relevant in this study. Also, empha-

sis was not on the age of the participants as all the participants were 18 years and above. The participants' coded used
in the study were presented in the table below.

The participant demographics was a crucial aspect of this
research because of the qualifications needed for participation
in the study. The participants in the study were evenly divided into Faith-Based Leaders (FBLs) and Non-Faith-Based
Leaders (NFBLs). The participants' demographics presented
in this chapter was not a detailed demographic data normally
added in the appendix. The demographics were simply to
highlight the qualification of the participants for the study
based on the recruitment criteria. Information about the participants' gender was not relevant in this study. Also, emphasis was not on the age of the participants as all the
participants were 18 years and above. The participants' coded
used in the study were presented in the Table 2 below.

Table 2
Participants' Codes

Faith-Based Leaders	Non-Faith-Based Leaders
P1FBL	P8NBL
P2FBL	P9NBL
P3FBL	P10NBL
P4FBL	P11NFBL
P5FBL	P12NFBL
P6FBL	P13NFBL
P7FBL	P14NFBL

The table above represented the codes used in describing
the study participants for the confidentiality of their data. All
other aspects of the participants' demographics needed in the
study where discussed in piecemeal to ensure the privacy of
the participants. All the participants met the necessary educa-

tional qualification of a bachelor degree and above. All the participants in faith-based and non-faith-based also met their initial leadership experience measured in years of leadership and staff strength. All the FBLs also met the congregation membership strength of 20 and above. The NFBLs alike met their staff strength of five workers minimum under their supervision. All the participants, faith-based and non-faith-based were located in the city of Richmond, Virginia as of the time of the study.

The tabulated information relating to the educational qualifications of the both the FBLs and the NFBLs were presented in Table 3 below.

Table 3.
Educational Qualifications of FBLs & NFBLs

Educational Levels	Frequency	Percentage (%)
Bachelors	5	36%
Masters	6	43%
Doctorates	3	21%

Based on the prequalification criteria for the study, all the respondents met the educational qualification needed to participate in the study. Out of the 14 respondents, five of them had a bachelor degree representing 36%. Six of the 14 participants had a master degree representing 43%. Only three of the 14 members, had doctorate representing 21%. A minimum qualification of 4 years bachelor degree was required to qualify for the study. The qualification frequencies were graphically presented in figure next.

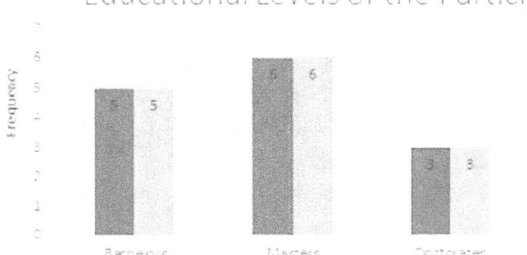

Educational Levels of the Participants

Figure 2: Graphical Description of the Participants Qualifications

The chart above indicated that the commonest educational qualifications of the participants was master's degree. Only three participants representing 21% had a doctorate degree. The remaining 36% of the participants had bachelors. The tabulated information relating to the years of leadership of both the FBLs and the NFBLs were presented in Table 4 below.

Table 4

Years of Leadership of FBLs & NFBLs

Years of Engagement	Frequency	Percentage (%)
6-10	8	57%
11-15	4	29%
16-20	2	14%

All the respondents met the required engagement years of at least three years. Exploring the participants' years of leadership was necessary for this research to make certain that the leaders occupied the position for a reasonable period. Eight out of the 14 participants representing 57%, were in the position between six to 10 years. Four out of the 14 participants representing 29% were in the position between 11-15 years. Only two of the 14 members were in the position between 16-20 years representing 14%. The experience frequencies were graphically presented in the figure below.

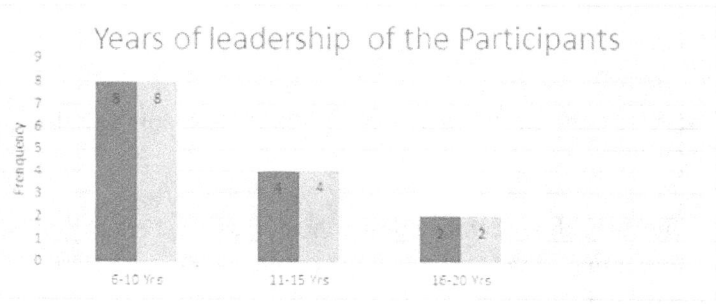

Figure 3: Graphical Description of the Participants' Experiences

The charts above indicated that the longest leadership experience of participants were 16-20 years (14%), but the commonest leadership experience of participants were 6-10 years (57%). The participants with the second longest leadership experience were 11-15 years (29%). The tabulated information relating to the membership strength of the FBLs were presented in Table 5 next.

Table 5

Membership Strength of the FBLs

Membership Strength	Frequency	Percentage (%)
40-60	2	29%
120-140	3	43%
480-500	1	14%
520-540	1	14%

Adequate membership strength of the FBL was a criterion for participation in this study. A minimum of 20 members were required for a FBL to take part in the study. Adequate membership was necessary to measure the leadership experience of the FBL. Out of seven FBLs, two of them had a membership strength of 40-60 members in their faith-based organization representing 29%. Three FBLs had a membership strength of 120-140 members representing 43%. One FBL had a membership strength of 480-500 members representing 14%. Only one FBL had the highest congregational membership of 520-540 representing 14%. The membership strength frequencies of the FBLs were graphically presented below.

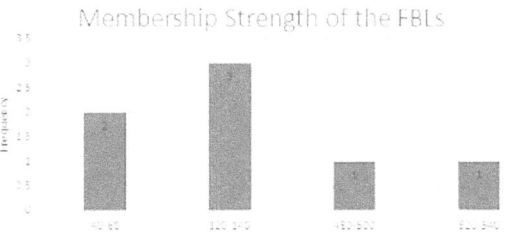

Figure 4: Graphical Description of the Membership Strength of the FBLs

The above charts revealed that only one participant representing 14% of the FBLs had the highest congregational membership of 520-540. The participants with the commonest membership strength of 120-140 were 43%. The tabulated information relating to the staff strength of the NFBLs were presented in Table 6 below.

Table 6

Staff Strength of the NFBLs

Staff Strength	Frequency	Percentage (%)
6-10	3	43%
11-15	1	14%
16-20	2	29%
111-115	1	14%

Adequate staff strength of the NFBL was a criterion for participation in this study. A minimum of five staff under the supervision of a NFBL was required for participation in the study. Out of the seven NFBLs in the study, three of them had a staff strength of between six-10 staff representing 43%. One out of the seven NFBLs had a staff strength of between 11-15 representing 14%. Two of the seven NFBLs had a staff strength of between 16-20 staff representing 29%. Only one NFBL had a staff strength of between 111-115 staff representing 14%. The staff strength frequencies of the NFBLs were graphically presented next.

Figure 5: Graphical Description the Staff Strength of the NFBLs

The above charts revealed that only one participant representing 14% of the NFBLs had the highest staff strength of 111-115 workers. But 6-10 workers were the most common number of workers supervised by the NFBLs. The tabulated information relating to the current position of the both the FBL and the NFBL were presented in Table 7 below.

Table 7
Current Positions of the FBLs & NFBLs

Current Positions	Frequency	Percentage (%)
President	3	21%
Senior Pastor	2	14%
Directors	5	36%
Associates/Assistants	4	29%

Holding an executive position such as a President, CEO, Director, Senior Pastor, and Assistant Manager was required for participation in this study. These positions were necessary to measure the leadership experience on a face value. Out of the 14 participants in the study, only three held the position of a president representing 21%. Two of the participants held a senior pastor's position representing 14%. Five of the participants were in the directorship positions representing 36%. Four participants were in the associates or assistants position representing 29%. The position frequencies of the FBLs and the NFBLs were graphically presented below.

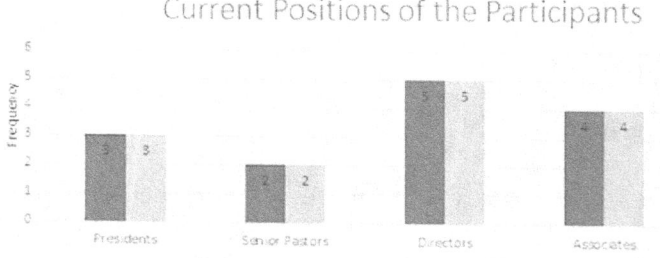

Figure 6: Graphical Description of the Current Positions of Participants

The above charts indicated that the most common positions occupied by the study participants were directors while senior pastors took the least position. Other positions were somewhat evenly distributed. The tabulated information relating to the age bracket of the FBLs and NFBLs were presented in Table 8 below.

Table 8
Age Bracket of the FBLs & NFBLs

Age Brackets	Frequency	Percentage (%)
35-40	1	08%
40-45	3	21%
45-50	6	43%
50-55	2	14%
55-60	2	14%

The table above (page 100) represent the age brackets of the participants in the study. Information about the participants' age was not the focus of this research because all the respondents met the age requirement of 18 years. A tabulation of the participants' age bracket was still necessary to present the age levels of participants in the study. Out of 14 respondents, only one was in the age range of between 35-40 representing 8%. Three out of the 14 members representing 21% were in the age bracket of 40-45. Participants with the highest frequency of six representing 43% were in the age bracket of 45-50. Two members out of 14 representing 14% were within the age bracket of 50-55. Only two participants were within the age range of 55-60 representing 14%. The age bracket frequencies of the FBLs and the NFBLs were graphically presented below.

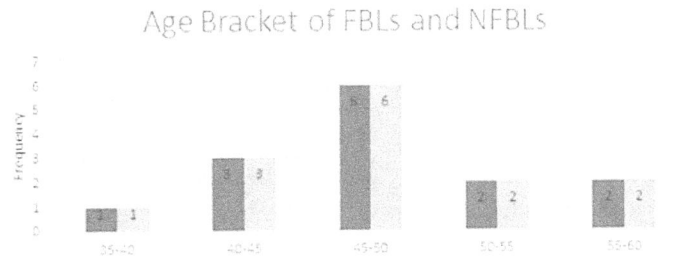

Figure 7: Graphical Description of the Age Bracket of Participants

The above charts indicated the highest participants' age range of 45-50 years while the lowest was 35-40 years. Other age ranges were somewhat evenly spread. The next section will be used for data analysis.

Data Analysis

The data analysis of the study started during the data collection where detail notes were taken. The researcher adopted Seidman's three interview phases where phase one was used to prescreened the respondents. The first six interview questions were used to explore the qualifications of the interviewees during the phase one of Seidman interviews. The first six interview questions were based on the recruitment criteria (residency in Richmond, basic academic qualification, leadership experiences, etc.). The Seidman's Interviews Phase One (The Prescreening Phase) was used to prescreened 45 volunteers using the phone. Out of 45 screened volunteers, 38 were qualified for participation, but nine dropped out. Out of the remaining 29 screened volunteers, 14 were selected for the second phase of Seidman's interviews.

The interviews scripts of Seidman's phase two were the actual interviews analyzed in the study. Seidman's interviews phase three was only used to play back the responses of the respondents for ratification. At the end of the interview process, the audio files were transcribed using the Microsoft words and was adequately reviewed several times and verified by each participant before analysis. The transcripts were exported chronologically for ease of coding into NVivo10. The first seven transcripts exported were those of FBLs followed by those of the NFBLs. The transcripts were exported in this fashion for the ease of classification, categorization, and coding. The classification of the data by sorting and coding were the primary process of analyzing the data of the study.

The initial process of data classification and categorization was done through auto coding of the interview transcripts based on the interview questions. The auto coding queries were done by entering all the interview questions and participants' responses in the NVivo10. Before running the queries, the interview questions and the answers were marked for identification. All the interview questions were marked with level one word type, and all the responses were marked with level two word type. The reason for differentiating the dataset with level one and level two was to help the researcher in the data identification. At the end of the queries, responses of all the participants from the interviews were grouped according to question numbers.

The queries resulted in the emergence of three data categories as follows:

1) Perceptions of EI,

2) 21st Century Leadership Environment

3) Stress and People Management Strategies.

The three categories were broken into seven descriptive themes. The themes were later streamlined to five based on their capabilities to answer the research questions and research problem as follows:

1) Theme #1- How the NPO leaders perceive the construct of EI or what EI mean to NPO leaders (generated from category one).

2) Theme # 2- How the environment of NPOs is sensitive and volatile for leadership in the 21st-century (generated from category 2).

3) Theme # 3- How the NPO leaders walk away briefly from the environment of stress as a coping strategy (generated from category 3)

4) Theme # 4-How the NPO leaders practice self-control

with team members Or How they act in a professional
manner as a conflict control approach (generated from
category 3)
5) Theme #5- How the NPO leaders practice respect for
team members for team harmony (generated from category 3)

Another categorization process took the form of word
cloud, word tree, and word search. The word cloud and word
tree assisted in presenting a visualized versions of the most
frequent words used by the respondents. The most common
words helped the researcher to articulate the focus of the interviewees and why. The data were re-coded to check the
connectedness and differentiation of responses.

Overview of Findings from the Interview Questions
The following were the responses of the participants based
on the interview questions. For the purpose of this study, the
analysis was based only on the Seidman's phase two interviews (the actual interviews that explore the professional experiences of the participants). Seidman phase one interviews
were used only to screened and recruit participants into the
study. The only question that was repeated in the phase one
and two of the Seidman's interviews was questions number
six of the prescreening period. This prescreening question
number six became question number one in the Seidman's interviews Phase 2.

Interview Question #1. *"What is EI to you?"*
The primary purpose of this question was to explore the
underlying knowledge of the respondents about EI. Although

the conceptual posture of EI was not expected from the interviewees, four out of the 14 respondents representing 29%, presented a conceptual approach to EI. Participant-P2FBL, stated that "EI is the ability of one to manage his emotion and other people's feelings to make them better and fruitful."

Participant P4FBL stated "EI is the capacity to understand your emotion and the feelings of others" P4FBL added, EI is the psychobiological bases of people's behavior. P4FBL maintained that people are always biased in their behavior. P4FBL concluded that in relating to people, you need to know their emotions and your feelings at the same time so that you will not take a rash leadership decision. Participant-P5FBL added another conceptual dimension as follows: "EI is the ability to master your emotion and be able to reason through issues instead of allowing your emotion to take control."

Some respondents offered a common-sense approach or a practical knowledge of EI. Example, Paticipant-P9NFBL stated that "EI is when you can separate your emotion from your work, and when you know when to use emotion in your job." Participant-P13NFBL presented something very broad by stating that "EI is the filter to which we process our whole world and store all the experiences of our world" The perspective of P13NFBL was wider in scope, and an attempt to get a simplified view was not successful.

Based on the broad and abstract nature of EI construct, a practical knowledge of EI was expected. Nine out of the 14 participants representing 64%, presented a practical knowledge of EI. However, one out of the entire participants representing 07%, demonstrated a moderate or low knowledge of EI in comparison to others. Example, A participant stated that

"EI is the approach to things, how you perceive something and approach it" Although no right or wrong answers were required, this response sounded a bit off the horizon of what EI is about.

Interview Question #2. *"Given the delicate nature of leadership duties in the 21st century, how would you foresee the role of emotional skills in leadership?"*

EI is paramount in the 21st century's leadership" The purpose of this question was to explore deeper into the emotional skills of the participants. Several thought provoking responses were generated from members. All the members representing 100% agreed that emotional skills are foreseeable under the leadership of 21st-century organizations. Several participants cited the sensitive leadership environment; some stressed the indispensability of emotional skills while some cited the sophisticated nature of 21st century's workforce as the basis for EI in leadership.

Interestingly, participant-P14NFBL stated that clients in the for-profit or NPOs may resort to technology as an alternative to toxic or leaders with low EI. P14NFBL stressed that people now have options to avoid poor client relations with the introduction of mobile apps (applications). Example, new technology (Periscope) can assist a person to hear the Gospel live anywhere without necessarily going to the church, thereby avoiding a minister with poor relationship skills. Participant-P12NFBL stated "Without emotional stability one cannot lead an organization, even in the leadership of a church" P12NFBL added, NPO leaders in particular who deals with volunteers have greater need of EI to get them to stay and give supports.

Interview Question #3. *"Assuming you have a stressful day at work because of workload or other inconveniences, how would you manage your stress to avoid transferring the aggression to others?"*

The purpose of this question was to explore the participants' stress management skills. Participants discussed different stress coping mechanism. Words such as calm-down, trigger, slow-down, and isolate where the frequently used words in this question. Participant-P12NFBL offered a sophisticated measure to deal with stress by saying "First of all, identify the trigger of the stress, sometimes overworking may not be the trigger of the stress but something else."

P12NFBL added that positive self-talk was a good way to deal with stress. P12NFBL concluded that verbalization helps one to vent out or offload the negative effect of stress. A critical assessment of all the approaches to managing stress indicated an inclination to the scientific module of stress management (taking a deep breath, taking a walk, etc.). Out of the 14 participants (FBL & NFBL), 13 of them representing 93% opted out for taking a walk and taking a deep breath as a coping mechanism. Only one out of the 14 participants representing 7%, subscribed to the help of the Holy Spirit in dealing with stress.

Interview Question #4. *"Assuming you encounter an annoying co-worker or client, how will you handle such a person?"*

The purpose of this question was to explore the relationship management skills or self-control skills of the participants. This problem was approached differently by the respondents. Three out of the 14 participants representing 21%, agreed to find out why the person is annoying or acting up. Two out of the 14 participants representing 14% agreed that they will tell-off the annoying person. Three out of 14 participants representing 21% accepted to avoid the annoying person. Six out of the 14 participants representing 43% agreed to use a professional behaviors or self-control by setting boundaries to deal with the annoying person. The common words used in this question were, avoid, nerves, people, deal, and emotion.

Interview Question #5. *"Assuming you are called upon to head a high performing team in your workplace, but the team members seem unwilling to follow rules because they are experts themselves?" How would you lead this type of workforce, and what skill would you use?"*

The purpose of this question was to explore the relationship management skills of participants. A good relationship manager should be able to break into the heart of difficult people skillfully to achieve the organizational goals. This question evoked varieties of responses. Six out of 14 participants representing 43%, suggested respect to team members as the best antidote to securing loyalty. In this same category, participant-P6FBL proposed the creation of a team of equals by seeing the team leader as equal with members. Participant-P12NFBL saw leadership as what you earned not your position or title.

Two out of the 14 participants representing 14% suggested the used of the passive-avoidance style of leadership where members take the lead while the team leader stays inactive. A member in this category wondered whether accepting a team leadership position will be an option in the first place. Five out of the 14 participants representing 36% favored appealing to the authority of their position to compel team members to cooperate. Only one out of the 14 participants representing 7% considered an outright resignation if unity is not achievable. Although, nine out of the14 participants representing 64% suggested the used of positions power as the last resort, only the 36% opted for position power as the first option.

Interview Question #6. *"Supposing you are in a position to take a challenging leadership decision that requires the contribution of ideas, how would you collate ideas appropriately and what skill would you use?"*

This question was also aimed at exploring the relational skills of participants. The question also sought the shared leadership skills of participants. This question was like the B part of question #5. Two of the 14 members repeated their responses to question #5. 100% of the participants agreed to seek the opinion of others using surveys, drop boxes, and meetings. Participant-P4FBL also decided to seek the advice of others and also the help of the Holy Spirit in making a decision. Participant-P5FBL supported sampling of ideas by saying "a leader with pre-conceived ideas will not open up to the views of others, and will always make a mediocre decision."

Interview Question #7. *"Assuming EI knowledge is critical to your leadership effectiveness, how would you share the experience with people in your industry or people around you?"*

The initial purpose of this question was to explore the participants' perceptions of EI. The secondary objective was to

study the value of EI to the leadership strategies of the participants. 100% of the participants agreed to share the knowledge with their associates for a harmonious relationship and
organizational development. Participant-P4FBL stated "it is a
must to share the knowledge" P4FBL supported with the
Bible reference "what you have heard me teach publicly you
should teach to others."

Emerging Themes

The analysis of the data of the study resulted in the emergence of three categories that were reduced to five themes
(parent nodes). The categories were Perceptions of EI, 21st
Century Leadership Environment, and Stress and People
Management Strategies. The groups were generated by con-
sidering the most common keywords and common phrases
used by the participants. The five themes made from the three
categories were considered based on its capability to answer
the research questions and to solve the research problem.
NVivo10 was used to classify and categorized the data from
which the themes emerged. The five themes enumerated
above were discussed in details as follows:

Theme #1: *The NPO leaders' perceptions about the term
EI.* Theme #1 was generated from interview question #1.
Question #1 was a crucial question in this study because of it
aims at exploring the basic knowledge of participants about
EI. The participants perceived EI in different ways. Although
no right or wrong answers were required, the varieties of the
responses revealed the subjective perceptions of participants
about EI. In comparison with the definition of EI by EI theorists, 29% of the respondents indicated a conceptual percep-

tion of EI, 64% of the interviewees reported a practical or common sense knowledge. Only 7% of respondents demonstrated a moderate or low perception of EI.

Participant-P2FBL stated EI is the ability for one to manage his emotion and other people's feeling to make them better and successful. P2FBL added "you need to control your emotion in order not to transfer the aggression to others" Paticipant-P3FBL on the other hand, stated EI is how you process your emotions as it relates to leadership. It has to do with working with others sharing or caring vision, how you handle the conversation. EI is the competency that allows you to handle emotional obstacles.

Participant-P4FBL stated "EI is the ability to look beyond just your views, to consider all the factors; EI is the capacity to understand your emotion and the feelings of others." It is the psychology behind people's behavior. People are always biased in their behavior. In relating to people, you need to know what your emotion and their feelings are at the same time so that you will not make a rash decision as a leader. Participant-P5FBL maintained that EI has to do with one's ability to master one own emotion and be able to reason through issues instead of merely allowing your feelings to take control. P5FBL added people of faith should be able to understand a lot about EI because of their need to control emotions.

Participant-P6FBL was of the opinion that EI is the ability to apply emotion to be able to have a handle and not allow emotion to have the better part of you. EI has to with learning how to react to things, words, behavior or attitudes towards you, that provoke you or naturally will cause you to act in a particular manner. Participant-P8NFBL, on the other hand, perceived EI from the perspective of a kid. P8NFBL said EI is like a child reacting appropriately to emotion. EI is also the ability of a child to recognize the feelings of other children and relate to them properly. Participant-P13NFBL approached EI from a holistic point of view. P13NFBL said EI is the filter to which we process our whole world and store all the experiences of our world emotionally, intellectually, and physically. P13NFBL added EI is what makes us human; it is part and parcel of us.

Participant-P12NFBL perceived EI as the ability of an individual to manage emotion to the extent that it minimizes negative emotions and enforce the positive one. Negative emotions such as stress and anxiety need to be put in control so that the positive one may thrive. Participant-P9NFBL perceived EI as the ability to separate your emotion from your work, and when people know when to use emotion in your job. One participant displayed a low or moderate EI perception by saying EI is how someone relate to things or the approach to things, how one perceive something and approach it.

Theme #2: *The leadership atmosphere of organizations in the 21stcentury is sensitive and volatile.* Another theme that gives credibility to the study was theme #2. The idea emerged from interview question #2. Nearly all the participants made reference directly or indirectly to the sensitive leadership environment. Participant-P2FBL referred to sensitive leadership situation from the angles of diversity, generational gap, age, and sexual orientation. P2FBL stated EI will forever remain a factor to attend excellence and to attend top goals. EI helps a leader to lead people from different generational categories, lifestyles, sexual orientation, and age. Participant-P1FBL referenced sensitive leadership environment as follows, the rights of the people, the awareness of individuals about their rights, and democracy made emotional skills foreseeable in the 21st-century leadership.

In a similar tone, Participant-P8NFBL said "in the society of today people need explanation about anything, you can't just say this thing happened, you must explain how and why it happened." P8NFBL added if you do not have the right emotion to answer those questions then you may be hurting people's feeling the more. P8NFBL concluded people are emotional and angry, and nobody knows why. Participant-P9NFBL stated because of the dynamic nature of the workforce; you cannot do without emotion.

Participant-P10NFBL referenced sensitive leadership environment by saying that the 21st century is getting more sophisticated, then you cannot rule out the role of EI in leadership. The choice of the word sophisticated here is synonymous with the complicated, indicating that the leadership environment of the 21st century is complicated. Participant-P5FBL echoed the sophisticated leadership environment as follows, in the current time, in the church or anywhere, we are dealing with complicated issues. P5FBL concluded your ability to empathize with people with different views and ideas determines your ability to be their leader.

Participant-P3FBL referenced the sensitive leadership environment as follows: In the 21st century, people have many distractions, an emotionally intelligent leader will be the right person to accommodate those distractions while leading people appropriately. Participant-P14NFBL referenced sensitive leadership environment by stressing the choice the followers can make based on their sensitivity. According to P14NFBL, with the introduction of mobile apps, people now have the option to avoid a weak EI leaders. Example, new technology (Periscope) can assist people to hear the Gospel live anywhere without necessarily going to the church, thereby avoiding a minister with low EI.

Theme #3: *The NPO leaders practice short walking away from the place of stress as a coping strategy.* Walking away briefly was the most common approach adopted by respondents as a stress management mechanism. Walking away was a parent node generated from question #3. Nine out of 14 participants representing 64% chose a little walking away from the stressful environment. Participant-P1FBL stated he or she will suspend everything and take a rest. P1FBL rather postponed the issue, or transfer the assignment to another. P1FBL rather take a break no matter how critical the issue is otherwise will transfer the aggression to someone else.

Similarly, Participant-P11NFBL handled the stress individually. P11NFBL stepped back from the situation and step out briefly. Participant-P13NFBL seemed more relax and taking charge of the stressful situation. P13NFBL always put into perspective the life events and not let one event define his or her life. P13NFBL always take a deep breath and always put himself or herself back in the center of his or her circle. P13NFBL always walk away, postpone some engagement and return when better. Participant-P14NFBL adopted a more professional approach to stepping away from the situation. P14NFBL try to leave the environment of stress mentally to a stress-free environment. P14NFBL try to stay calm to avoid the stress taking the better part of him or her. He or she used professional skills to avoid transferring the aggression to someone else.

According to participant-P12NFBL, identification of the stress trigger is the first thing to do. P12NFBL accepted walking away briefly as one of the stress coping mechanism but insisted that positive self-talk or verbalization is the best way to deal with stress. P12NFBL maintained that verbalization helps one to vent out or offload the negative effect of stress. Participant-P8NFBL agreed with P12NFBL on verbalization but insisted that walking away or isolation is the first step to addressing stress. Participant-P6FBL supported the recognition of stress trigger, also supported walking away, but recommended delegation of duties as the best way to emotional relieve.

Theme #4: *The NPO leaders practice self-control with team members to manage conflict.* The Practice of self-control or acting in a professional manner by NPO leaders was a significant theme that revealed a person's EI. Among the five themes, practicing self-control was a more accurate skill in gauging a person's EI than others. The interviews revealed that some respondents actively and consistently practiced self-control in an emotionally charged atmosphere while some openly demonstrated the lack thereof.

Practicing self-control or acting in a professional manner emerged from questions #4, 5, & 6. There was a thin line between the outright practice of self-control and acting in a professional manner. Acting in a professional manner is a crucial aspect of practicing self-control. Differentiating self-control from acting in a professional manner was difficult but the researcher was able to spot out minor differences. 50% of the participants practiced an outright self-control while 43% demonstrated a professional behavior, only 7% leaned more to professionalism which may tilt a little toward poor self-control.

Eight participants displayed an outright restraint. What qualified respondents to this category was their patience in finding out what causes the annoyance of the upset person? A participant said he or she will find out why the person is annoyed and try to deal with the problem if possible. The participant said if the person is throwing a tantrum or is attacking, avoiding him will be the right decision to take. P4FBL said the first thing to do is to try to understand why the person is angry or annoyed. You will need to find out what is the psychology behind what the person is doing? P4FBL concluded knowing where this person is coming from in term of the sources, or the genesis of the problem will help in making this person relate to you.

Similarly, P9NFBL used professionalism to deal with the annoying person. P9NFBL gave them the opportunity to express themselves regarding what is going on with them. P9NBL empathized with them and refused to get mad. P10NFBL agreed to walk away from the situation that triggers strong emotion, but decided to find out what annoys the person. P10NFBL also displayed self-control based on the response that humility is the major factor in gaining the support of team members. P11NBL also demonstrated restraint by agreeing to call an annoying student outside for a talk. P11NFBL also decided to speak to a co-worker one-on-one. P13NFBL said the first thing to do is to find out what is going on with the person, why the person is acting this way. P2FBL also displayed self-control by calling the person to the office for a talk, suppressing anger, and drawing from the person's past positive behaviors.

The responses of four participant were categorized under professional attitudes. Acting in a professional manner was a good way to demonstrate self-control and EI, but it was not as empathic as displaying outright self-control in terms of being tolerant and patience with the annoying person. According to P3FBL, you need to manage them with the proper job description and role clarity and bring the mission back front and center. The job description should be the focal point to bring us back to focus. P3FBL said one need to make it clear that annoying behavior is not acceptable, and a recurring event may lead to a correcting action such as query or termination.

A participant said dealing with an irritating person calls for "not fainting on the day of adversity." You do not have absolute control of how people behave. Therefore, it is wrong to be soaked by the emotional instability of someone else. Your EI knowledge should help you to know that you were not the cause of the problem. The EI knowledge will also help you navigate your way out of the problem. P6FBL noted that the conventional thing is to avoid an annoying person, but agreed that it will be counter-productive to do so. P6FBL also deal with the upset person professionally and try not to get annoyed by him. P6FBL may also try to be friendly with the person to win his acceptance. According to P6FBL, the ability to trivialize or ignore some matters and move on may help.

A participants acted too professionally leaning a little toward low tolerance to some behaviors. Although being EI is not a reason to agree with everything, there is a thin line between agreeability and being empathetic and sympathetic.

117

The participant said he or she will talk to the annoying person about how his behavior is affecting the participant. Also, apply "positive self-talk" i.e., voicing out your unwillingness to be moved by the antic of the annoying person is another good option to apply. Also, letting the irritating person know that he or she cannot define you is good way to deal with stress.

Theme #5: *The NPO leaders practice respect for team members for team harmony.* The last theme that emerged during the analysis was respect for team members or co-worker. This topic emerged from interview questions #4 & #5. Nine participants demonstrated a great sense of respect for their team members and co-workers in one way or the other representing 64%. A display of respect for people below your level, people in your payroll, or people you can easily boss around is a true display of emotional strength. According to one FBL, the first thing to do is to respect them as individuals and professionals. You must also know what to do before you are respected. Take time to appreciate them and remind them that you are not only a team leader but also a member of the team. Highlight the importance of the team objective more than your title. After doing all you supposed to do and some are still not ready to cooperate, the best is to take them out of the group.

Another FBL came up with a thought-provoking approach. According to this leader, creating a team of equals where the leader will not operate as the head will be the approach. This FBL will assign duties in such a way that everyone is relevant to the team. In other words, the leader made everyone a co-leader of the team. A NFBL saw leadership as what you earned not your position or title. According to this leader, leadership is not a title or position but it is what you earned. Being appointed a team leader does not make you a leader but gives you the opportunity to gain leadership through practice. The leader offered to create a time to talk to team members one-on-one to win them back to the team if feeling rejected. The managed emotion and try not to take it personally.

Four participants demonstrated servant leadership in the ways they showed respect to their team members. According to one NFBL, humility is the key factor; you do not have to be too bossy. To garner their cooperation, you have to come to their level. Your manner of presentation matters and you have to be sympathetic and empathetic. Another NFBL said he or she will honestly solicit help from them to make the team assignment a success. He or she will cooperate, share, and be honest with the team for team spirit.

A FBL added as a child of God, wherever you find yourself show respect to anybody who come your way. This FBL used communication skills to target their area of strength to secure cooperation. P9NFBL allowed team members to make suggestions based on their experiences, and P9NBL looked at those suggestions to make decisions. P9NBL tried as much as possible to see things from the follower's point of view, especially sound ideas. P9NBL respect the follower and do not waste away experiences.

P7FBL showed regards to team members by opening up and embracing their ideas before making group decisions. But, P14NFBL, sets the rules for respect to everybody. According to P14NFBL, "we have to set rules to be respectful to each other, and everybody have to obey the rules." The decision to come down to the level of the team members and co-workers to respect them was found to be a smooth way to create team spirit. Although 70% of the participants had staff discipline in mind as their backup, they attempted the civilize approach (respect) first. The next section will be used to present a comparative overview of the responses of the FBLs and NFBLs.

A Comparative Overview of the FBLs and the NBLs

The responses of the FBLs and the NFBLs based on the theoretical and common sense definitions of EI did not reveal any significance differences. Comparatively, both the FBLs and the NFBLs demonstrated adequate knowledge of EI. The knowledge or perceptions of EI was categorized into three groups (Conceptual Knowledge, Commonsense or Practical Knowledge, and Moderate or Low Knowledge). The conceptual understanding group were those who perceived or defined EI theoretically similar to or according to the EI theorists. The common sense or practical knowledge group were those who demonstrated the core or layman's knowledge of EI or displayed a sound understanding of what EI is all about. The moderate or low perception group were those whose perception were below those of the common sense and the conceptual levels. Table below presents a comparative overview of the perceptions of FBLs and the NFBLs. See Table 9.

EI Levels of Perception	FBLs	NFBLs
Conceptual Perceptions	3	0
Practical Perceptions	3	7
Low Perceptions	1	0

Note. FBLs= Faith-Based Leaders, NFBLs= Non-Faith-Based Leaders.

The table above indicated the EI perceptions of both the FBLs and the NFBLs. Although no right or wrong answers were required, the high conceptual perceptions of EI by FBLs and the great practical perceptions of the NFBLs complemented each other showing no significant differences. One low EI perception by a FBL also supplemented by the zero conceptual and zero moderate perceptions by the NFBLs.

The FBLs were observed to be stricter in their approach to staff discipline than their NFBLs' counterpart. The observation is subject to further research. Interview questions 4 and 5 were used as the basis of the remark. The comment was necessary given the leadership problem plaguing the nonprofit sector. Four FBLs, expressed their intolerance for recalcitrant workers. According to one FBL, you need to manage them with the proper job description and role clarity and bring the mission back front and center. The job description should be the focal point to bring everybody back to focus. You need to make it clear that annoying behavior is not acceptable, and a recurring event may lead to a correcting action such as queries or termination. The same participant also opted to resign from the team leadership if team members refuse to cooperate.

Similarly, another FBL responded to the annoying coworker as follows, being a child of God is not a license to be taken for a ride. The same participant responded as follows about a rebellious team member: When leadership mandate is on you, it makes you a leader. You follow the rules and regulations, speak to them first and see whether they will change, but if they refuse you write them up and discipline them. Another FBL followed the same pattern about an annoying person as follows: After trying all the options and the person still do not change, take him out so as not to spoil others. Another FBL also followed the same pattern of discipline on rebellious team members.

But, four NFBLs, demonstrated some levels of tolerance to the annoying person and the un-cooperating team members. One of the four said, leadership is earned not acquired. Another demonstrated servant leadership through showing humility, respect, and empathy for the unruly team members. Another NFBL displayed servant leadership by going all out to appeal for help from an un-cooperating team member. All these soft attitudes were obviously absent among the FBLs. As a matter of fact, one FBL maintained that when a leadership mandate is on you, it makes you a leader. Evoking the leadership mandate indicated an unwillingness to tolerate anything out of order. Additional research about this observation is recommended. The next section, Chapter 5 will be used for the conclusion, summary, and recommendations.

Chapter Summary

The focus of chapter four was on the data analysis. The chapter started with a revisit of the research purpose and problem statement. Also revisited were the significance of the study, the research question, and the research design. The field test was conducted to validate the interview questions. The field test assisted in rephrasing some of the interview questions. The data collection procedure was based on the purposive sampling using Seidman's three phase interviews. The first interview phase was used to prescreened participants into the study, the second phase was used to explore the professional experiences of the participants. The third and final phase was used to play back or crosscheck the interview responses.

Out of the 45 screened volunteers, 14 were selected to participate in the study. The demographic information of participants was discussed in Chapter 4. The research participants were evenly divided into the FBLs and NFBLs. The relevant demographic data needed in the study were, academic qualifications, years of leadership, and membership or staff strength. The participants' gender was not necessary and was not collected. Only the participants' age range was obtained but not directly relevant.

In Chapter 4, the data analysis method of the study was discussed. The computer software (NVivo10) was the primary data analysis method. The transcribed interviews scripts were exported into NVivo10 for analysis resulting in the emergence of five themes. Also in chapter4, the seven interview questions and responses were reviewed. The research themes (NPO leaders' perceptions of EI construct, Sensitive leadership environment in the NPOs, Practicing self-control by NPO leader/Acting in a professional manner by NPO leader, Practicing respect for team members by NPO leaders, & walking away briefly from the environment of stress) were fully discussed. The figure next was used to present the five themes.

Figure 8. A flow chart of the emerging themes is an original design from the findings of the present study using Microsoft Word Art.

The five themes emerged from the three categories. Theme one was the cardinal theme of the study because it explored the conceptual and practical perceptions of EI construct. The concept of EI has been misconstrued by many including scholars. Most of the times, the EI construct has been mistaken as personality. Another issue was that most people may be high in EI but may not know anything about the construct. Theme one was used to exploring the real perceptions of EI among the NPO leaders. Other themes like theme number two, three, four, and five were used to access the application of EI by NPO leaders. A sound application of EI concept in the leadership revealed to a greater extent the actual perceptions of EI. Lastly, a comparative overview of the FBLs and NFBL were examined. The comparison was necessary based on the observed perceptions of the FBLs and the NFBLs.

Chapter 5
Conclusions and Recommendations

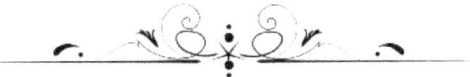

■ The findings from the present research highlighted the EI perceptions of NPO leaders. Some of the study results also validated the submissions of the literature reviewed in the study. The findings and implications of the study substantiated the five descriptive themes of the research. The findings demonstrated the current perceptions and understanding of participants about EI.

The emphatic statement by Goleman (1995) that EI cannot be done without by leaders remained something to ponder over by the present and future leaders. The leadership environment of the 21st century continued to stay slippery, fragile, fluid, volatile, and complicated (Hickman, 2010). Krell (2013) stressed the need for people-centered leadership with a sense of purpose in achieving business goals and objectives.

The current paradigm shift from cognitive and technical intelligence to emotional and social intelligence also bolster the need for research on EI (Manolis et al., 2009). But a review of the literature revealed that majority of studies conducted on the EI and leadership referenced to the for-profit organizations. This gap in literature propelled the researcher to do similar study on NPOs. Particularly, the famous theory that EI is indispensable to the leadership was needed to be examined in respect of the administration of NPOs (George et al., 2014).

The purpose of this qualitative descriptive inquiry was to explore NPO leaders' perceptions about the value of EI on leadership strategies in the City of Richmond, Virginia. The numerous values of EI in leadership asserted by scholars made the need to explore the NPO leaders' perceptions about EI crucial. The general business problem was the lack of emotionally competent leadership in the nonprofit sector resulting in high rate of fraud and scandals among the industry leaders globally (Ross, 2011). The particular business problem was the perceptions of the NPO leaders about the value of EI on leadership strategies in Richmond Virginia was unknown. Based on the unknown EI experience of the NPO leaders, the qualitative descriptive inquiry was a perfect approach to exploring the EI perceptions among the NPO leaders. The next section will be used to present an overview of the finding's summary.

Summary of the Findings of the Themes

The findings from the present research highlighted the EI perceptions of NPO leaders. Some of the study results also validated the submissions of the literature reviewed in the

study. The findings and implications of the study substantiated the five descriptive themes of the research. The findings
demonstrated the current perceptions and understanding of
participants about EI. The critical conclusion drawn from the
research findings revealed that participants broadly viewed EI
to refer to how they relate with people especially their subordinates and co-workers.

Theme #1: *The NPO leaders' perceptions about the term
EI:* Findings from this theme were grouped into three categories of EI perceptions by NPO leaders namely (a) conceptual or theoretical perceptions (b) practical or common sense
perceptions (c) moderate or low perceptions. The conceptual
EI perceptions pertained to the demonstration of theoretical
knowledge similar to those of EI theorist such as Goleman
(1995). The common sense EI perceptions related to the expression of practical or layman's views of EI. The moderate
or low EI perceptions related to the demonstration of weak
views of EI. The categorization was used to evaluate the participants' understanding of EI.

Both the conceptual group and the practical group representing 93% of the participants demonstrated adequate
knowledge of EI. The study findings are similar to the current
literature review findings of Tucker et al. (2000), which confirmed the conceptual perception of EI as a person's ability to
identify and react to emotions of oneself and the feelings of
others. This opinion highlighted the significance of identifying one's emotions first and the emotions of others. Failure to
take one's emotions and the emotions of others into consideration may be counterproductive because both sides of the
emotions matter in a harmonious relationship.

The literature review findings of Trautmann et al. (2007) also supported the theoretical perception of EI. According to Trautmann et al. (2007), EI can be perceived as the ability to discern one's emotions and the emotions of others, and to use the information to connect, communicate, and influence others. The identification of emotions from oneself first and the emotions of others helps in making sound judgement. According to Ramesh (2013), the high achieving leaders otherwise described as emotional leaders, continuously address the emotional needs of followers in an effort to secure optimum performance from them.

The literature review findings of Sakiru et al. (2013), supported the practical perceptions of EI. According to Sakiru et al. (2013), EI represents a variety of mental capabilities and skills that guides a person's power to manage the demand and stress of the environment. The findings of the practical perceptions of EI was also consistent with the literature review results of Iuscu, Neagu, and Neagu (2012), which posited that EI is a way of life. EI is the way we process our world in all ramifications. The commonsense perceptions of EI was also similar to the literature review results of Colfax, Rivera, and Perez (2010), who narrowed the description of a person's EI to possessing common-sense. No literature reviews were found to be similar to the moderate or weak perceptions of EI signifying that poor EI perceptions were off the horizon of EI research at the moment.

Theme #2: *The leadership atmosphere of organizations in the 21stcentury is sensitive and volatile:* The present study findings stressed the need of EI knowledge in the direction of the sensitive workforce of the current era. The research results were consistent with the literature review findings of Krell (2013). According to Krell (2013), the chaotic, fluidity and extreme volatile features of 21st-century organizations requires people centered leadership with a sense of purpose in achieving business goals and objectives. The leadership climate of the present era is hostile impeding the smooth direction and harmonious working atmosphere. Findings from the study indicated the societal demands for an explanation about every decision and action.

The sensitive, diverse, and enlightened clientele, especially in schools, churches, and hospitals, requires a thorough explanation about every incident that occurred on the premises of these organizations. This uncertain situation keeps leaders constantly on toes because of fear of lawsuits. The literature review findings of Neera et al. (2010) highlighted the enlightened society by stating "The illiteracy in the 21st-century does not imply the inability to read and write, but the inability to learn, unlearn, and relearn." (p. 21). The literature review findings of Hickman (2010), also corroborated with study findings on sensitive leadership environment. According to Hickman (2010), the volatile leadership environment of the 21st-century caused by the presence of more knowledgeable and delicate workforce suggests the relevance of EI in organizations' leadership.

Theme#3: *The NPO leaders practice short walking away from the place of stress as a coping strategy:* Among the numerous stress management strategies suggested by the NPO leaders, walking away briefly from the stressed environment was highlighted the most. The NPO leaders like their for-profit counterpart are confronted with stressful situations daily. The ability to deal with the stressful situation appropriately and timely was found to be the only way to save the day. The literature review findings of Ramesh (2013) stated why many people become bad tempered when stressed is because they have bad stress management abilities. Ramesh (2013) went ahead to recommend that possessing EI is the first step to stress management.

But findings from the NPO leaders indicated that identifying the right stress trigger is the first step to stress management. Although identifying the stress trigger is the right step in stress management but, possessing EI skills is needed to identify and align the trigger to a given stressful situation (Ramesh, 2013). Quite often than not, NPO leaders are always vulnerable to excessive stress because of their unclear or overly demanding work leading to burnout. According to Buys and Rothmann (2010), "Burnout, is conceptualized as a physiological syndrome in response to chronic interpersonal stressors on the job.

The literature review findings of Ramesh (2013) validated the findings of NPO leaders on stress management strategies. According to Ramesh (2013), "when you experience anger or other strong emotions, slow down to examine why" (p. 213). Slowing down or stepping away briefly from the stressful situation most of the time helps in cooling down the strong emotion as such saves someone from acting rashly. Ramesh (2013) maintained no matter the circumstance, you always have the power to decide how you react to it that will help you understand what your emotions are telling you.

Theme #4: *The NPO leaders practice self-control with team members to manage conflict:* One of the best ways to determine the EI knowledge of a person has to do with his/her regards to self-control or exhibition of professional attitude. Practicing self-control is a necessary if not a mandatory skill for all leader for-profits and non-profits inclusive. The literature review findings of Swanson, Andree, Bowler, Brand, Zobisch, and Paula (2014), validated the study's findings on practicing self-control. According to Swanson et al.(2014), "people who cannot control their emotions fight inner battles that sabotage their ability for focused work and clear thought"(p.45). Capacity to fight emotional battle in the face of emotional duress prevents an "emotional hijacking" where ones' emotions take over the entire experience and create a bigger situation than existed (Swanson et al., 2014, p.45).

The leadership of the organization in the present age needs emotionally sound leaders one who are capable of delaying the gratification of venting out feelings during an emotional crisis. According to Ramesh (2013), high achieving or EI leaders remain composed, untroubled, and collected in the process of leading. EI leaders also manage the feelings to react by either delaying or completely resisting reaction in the moment of a significant disruption in daily activities or calamity. Similarly, the literature review findings of Ingram and Cangemi (2012) maintained managers have the responsibility of controlling their state of mind and the emotions of employees whether convenient or not.

The study findings also aligned with the literature review findings of Swanson et al., (2014), who referenced Goleman (1995) as follows, "EI is the ability to encourage oneself and persevere in the moment of exasperation, to control feeling and postpone satisfaction, and to control one's moods" In a proverbial manner, the literature review findings of Ramesh

(2013) stated EI or high achieving leaders were builders not destroyers when life throws them curve-balls, they know that life is not without challenges, and everything can work together for good in the long run. The study findings indicated that NPO leaders have a higher need for self-control than their for-profit counterpart because of their predominance dependence of unpaid volunteers. It can be counterproductive venting anger on people who step in to help free of charge no matter the magnitude of their error.

Theme #5: *The NPO leaders practice respect for team members for team harmony:* The last theme that emerged during the data process was the need to respect co-workers or team members. Respect to anybody especially one below your rank displays one level of EI. The era of suppressive, coercive, and autocratic leadership has long gone (Wren, 2013). In the present era of workforce higher preference to shared or co-leadership, it takes an EI leader to share the benefit of an exalted position with others (ranks and files). The study findings corroborated with the literature review findings of Ramesh (2013) which said the decisions of the leader must incorporate the emotions of followers about the organization, the department, the culture and/or the project.

The leader who respect the feelings of the follower will take them into consideration when making decisions. Others (transactional leaders) will only focus and pursue the vision and goals of the organization at the detriment of the concerns of the followers. According to Ramesh (2013), leading follower emotions should take the primary attention of any organizational builder, corporate transformer or any person looking to leave a footprint in the company. The study findings on coworkers depicted the literature review findings on servant leadership. Servant Leadership is a leadership perspective where the leader's cardinal motive is to serve others (Goh & Low, 2014). As celebrated as transformational leadership is their bottom-line is organizational growth whereas the bottom-line of a servant leader is the growth of workers. NPO leaders have a higher need to respect the workforce because of their service to humanity motives of establishment and their predominant used of the voluntary workforce. The next section will be used to explore findings related to the two interview questions.

Findings Relating to RQ1

Findings from the five descriptive themes correlated with the RQ1. Technically, RQ1 was the overarching RQ of the study because it explored the central question of the study (NPO Leaders' Perceptions of EI). The primary theme that answered this question was theme#1. Findings from this theme revealed three categories of EI perceptions by NPO leaders namely (a) conceptual or theoretical perceptions (b) practical or common sense perceptions (c) moderate or low perceptions. The conceptual EI perceptions pertained to the demonstration of theoretical knowledge similar to those of the EI theorists. The common sense EI perceptions related to the expression of realistic or layman's views of EI. The moderate or low EI perceptions related to the demonstration of weak views of EI. The categorization was used to evaluate the participants' understanding of EI.

The findings related to RQI agreed with the literature review findings of Tucker et al., (2000), which confirmed the conceptual perceptions of EI as a person's ability to identify and react to emotions of oneself and the feelings of others. This perception reflected the importance of first identifying personal emotions then the emotions of others. According to Trautmann et al. (2007), EI can be perceived as the ability to discern one's emotions and the emotions of others, and to use the information to connect, communicate, and influence others.

Colfax et al.(2010) posited adequate perceptions of EI can be compared to the effective self-management and social dexterity. Kewalramani et al. (2015) warned that high EI perceptions are not the same thing as having EI competencies, but it is an indication that a person is capable of learning the EI skills. Findings from other themes also correlated to RQ1 as they revealed the how NPO leaders apply EI in their leadership. Many FBLs and NFBLs demonstrated sound EI perceptions in their leadership practice.

Findings Relating to RQ2

The purpose of this RQ was to examine and explore the perceptions of the FBLs compared with the perceptions of the NFBLs. Although both the FBLs and NFBLs are sub-divisions of the NPOs, the non-faith-based NPOs often have clear structure than the faith-based counterparts (Meyer & Taylor, 2013). The question was necessary because of the ongoing leadership dilemmas in nonprofits associated with employees discipline issues. According to McMurray (2010), the challenge of effective leadership in NPOs is the "spiritualization" of employee discipline issues (p. 436). The current study revealed that the FBLs were stricter in the employee discipline than their NFBLs' counterpart. Although the study result is subject to further research, the result indicated the FBLs are not taking staff discipline for granted as studies asserted.

The study also revealed that the FBLs demonstrated the conceptual or theoretical EI perceptions more than the NFBLs. The NFBLs on-the-other-hand demonstrated practical perceptions more than the FBLs. Displaying conceptual perceptions of EI may indicate high EI knowledge, but Kewalramani et al. (2015) warned high EI perceptions are not the same thing as having EI competencies, but it is an indication that the person is capable of learning the EI skills. The display of practical EI perceptions may be better than just having the knowledge of EI. According to Goleman (1995), having the EI skills or competencies is more rewarding than intelligent quotients. Iuscu et al. (2012) stated studies on EI offered a real platform to explore reasons some leaders are more skillful than others in their leadership strategies.

Limitations

The subjective nature EI construct was one of the hindrances that might have affected the responses of the participants. The study findings reported that only 29% of the participants viewed EI from the viewpoint of the EI theorists. 64% of the participants demonstrated their understanding of EI using their common sense while 7% applied extreme used of common sense showing a weak knowledge of EI. Another limitation of the study pertained to the voluntary nature of the study causing 24% of the screened volunteers to drop out. The voluntary nature of participant also made interviewing the 14 participants difficult.

Although interviews were supposed to be done at the convenience of the participants, securing the date, time, and venue of the meeting for two participants was harder because these members were very busy. Frankly speaking, one of them postponed the meeting seven times before I finally got hold of him. Another limitation was some NPO leaders were also doing their second jobs in the for-profit organizations; it was hard to decipher whether the source of their EI experience was from the for-profit or actually from the NPOs. Since the prequalification criteria did not include that the participants cannot have a second job in the for-profit organization, it is not known whether the result would have been different if participants did not have any link with for-profit organizations.

Implications

The implication of this research was divided into practical and theoretical as follows:

Practical implication/ implications of EI on leadership strategies. The implication of EI on leadership strategies has been researched by several researchers although no literature is found about EI and leadership strategies among NPO leaders. Among other researchers, Iuscu et al. (2012) noted that leaders high in EI are capable of promoting consistent production for the organization. Goleman et al. (2013) equated EI leaders to high achievers who balances budgets and ensure optimum production. Strategic leaders and indeed 21st leaders are highly adaptive and creative (Ross, 2012). In order to be creative and adaptive the role of EI cannot be rule out. The unclear or overly demanding work and lack of recognition which characterized NPO leaders made possessing EI and other personality traits inevitable for leadership success (Buys & Rothmann, 2010). Studies also indicated that high EI level leaders have less burnout rate and positive stress adaptation

(Estelle et al., 2013; Lopez-Zafra, 2015).

The importance of conducting this research was high based on the numerous values associated with EI by some scholars and researchers. Goleman (1995) notably asserted that EI cannot be done without by leaders. Based on Goleman's (1995) submissions, it was imperative to explore the awareness of the EI concept by nonprofit leaders. Possession of EI has been attributed to success in family, business, and life in general. The need to conduct the study among NPO leaders was nearly overdue. The allocation of 85% of human productivity or life success to emotional alertness or human engineering and only 15% to intellectual or IQ made this study more relevant and necessary.

Theoretical implications. The unknown EI perceptions among NPO leaders resulting in the adoption of descriptive inquiry made the present study of a theoretical significance. According to Purpose of Research (2015), a descriptive investigation is an effort to examine and explore the participants' experiences by describing the event in details and supplying the missing information for adequate comprehension. The description of the participant perceptions for clearer understanding and filling in the missing information is a clear indication that descriptive research is still at the exploratory stage capable of building new theories (Purpose of Research, 2015). The lack of literature review on EI and leadership among NPO leaders causing knowledge gap also created a theoretical implication for the current research. Although the primary purpose of the study was not to build theory or models, the contribution of the present research to future theoretical framework cannot be overestimated.

Recommendations

The recommendations of the current research were divided into two subdivisions as follows:

Recommendations for Leadership. The findings from the present study revealed some critical areas that for-profit or NPO leaders may need to address. The subjective nature of EI construct which caused people to view EI so differently, calls for a training program tailored toward the enlightenment of individuals about the theoretical construct of EI. The low or weak perception of EI by 7% of the participants highlighted the need for EI training among all the leaders in all divisions of NPOs. Based on the study findings that EI should be thoughts to all members of the organization for a harmonious relationship and overall organizational progress, EI training program should be organized for all members irrespective of position. Goleman et al. (2013) noted that EI cannot be done without by leaders. The implication is that EI is far greater than even the cognitive intelligence or IQ (Sadri, 2011).

A study conducted by the Carnegie Institute of Technology reveals 85% of a person's productivity is due to emotional alertness or human engineering, personality and ability to communicate, negotiate, and lead. But, only 15% percent is due to the intelligent quotient (Forbes Insights, 2012; Hahn et al., 2012). The good news to low EI people is EI can be trained, and EI improves as people grows older, unlike IQ that is limited by age (Goleman, 1995; Sadri, 2011). The diverse, volatile, and enlightened workforce in the 21st-century organizations for-profit or nonprofit has a greater need for EI leaders (Hickman, 2010). High achieving leaders or organizational performers with the potential to promote consistent output and organizational harmony are mostly high in EI

(Goleman et al., 2013; Iuscu et al., 2012).

Recommendations for Future Research. The purpose of this qualitative descriptive inquiry was to explore NPO leaders' perceptions about the value of EI on leadership strategies in the City of Richmond, Virginia. The adoption of descriptive research design which created a groundwork for a more conclusive future research made this study a stepping stone for future inquiry on EI and leadership among non-profit leaders (Purpose of Research, 2015). An overarching research question for the study was aimed at examining the EI perceptions by NPO leaders. But the second research question which compared the perceptions of the FBLs with that of the NFBLs revealed a profound result. The comparative overview of the two divisions of NPOs in the study showed that the FBLs were stricter in employee discipline than their NFBLs counterparts. This thought-provoking result evoked further studies as the findings conflicted with the mission and people focus of the faith-based NPOs usually characterized by over-spiritualization of employees' discipline issues (Cheverton, 2007; McMurray, 2010).

The mission-mindedness of the NPOs and their reliance on volunteers resulted in the NPOs' greatest dilemmas of poor leadership and weak organizational structure (Schoen-haus, 2002). There is a need to conduct a further research study to uncover (a) whether the FBLs themselves are competent in their leadership skills, but the mission focus of their organization weaken them regarding employee discipline? (b) whether the study result would have changed if the FBLs were compared with the for-profit leaders in the corporate world? (c) whether a context-based leadership training is needed for the FBLs that may make them mutually exclusive of other sectors.

According to Lindenberg (2001), the changing leadership focus in the 21st century and ongoing attraction to adopt the for-profit management strategies propelled some NPOs to consider the for-profit management strategies. Bunchapattanasakda et al. (2012) feared that the adoption may not work out in the long run because NPOs and for-profits have different motives. Finally, this study need to be replicated using the mixed methods research method for triangulation purposes and the geographical location of the study need to be expanded for adequate sampling and a more inclusive result.

Chapter Summary

Chapter 5 was used for the summary and conclusion of the research study with reference to the other four chapters. The overview of the study findings were summarized based on the emerging themes. Theme #1 was addressing the various EI perceptions of the participants. The variations in their perceptions were also discussed. Theme #2 addressed the sensitive leadership environment of the 21st century. The need for an EI leadership in managing the volatile leadership atmosphere were also highlighted. Theme #3 addressed stress management strategies suggested by participants. Walking away from the stressful environment was the common suggestion for stress management.

Theme #4 addressed the practice of self-control or acting in a professional manner as strategies to relating with a rebellious and annoying coworker. Lastly, theme #5 discussed respect for team members and coworkers as a sure way for harmonious coexistence among the workforce. Also discussed in chapter 5 was the limitations of the study. The practical and theoretical implications of the study was also discussed. In Chapter 5, the recommendations for leadership and future researchers were also discussed. Chapter 5 ended with the conclusion of the study with direct reference to answering the research question of the study.

Conclusions

The purpose of the current qualitative descriptive inquiry was to explore and examine the NPO leaders' perceptions about the value of EI on leadership strategies in the City of Richmond, Virginia. The research problem was the perceptions of the NPO leaders about the value of EI on leadership strategies in Richmond Virginia was unknown resulting in the training program decision dilemmas for the sector. The overarching research question for the study was: What are the perceptions of NPO leaders concerning the value of EI on leadership strategies in Richmond Virginia? In assessing the overarching research question, the participants' perceptions about EI was grouped into conceptual knowledge, common sense knowledge, and moderate knowledge.

The creative design of the interview questions was geared toward unveiling the EI perceptions of the NPO leaders. The study findings revealed that EI was not new to NPO leaders. Although not 100% of the participants demonstrated the theoretical and practical perceptions of EI, the overall conclusion about their EI perceptions indicated that a substantial percentage of NPO leaders had EI awareness. The findings from the second research question revealed that the FBLs were stricter than the NFBLs in the employee discipline. The result from the RQ2 called for future research to verify the findings.

Based on the study findings that about 64% of NPO leaders had practical perceptions of EI and the fact that EI is a relatively new conceptual construct, need to initiate appropriate EI training programs will be a step in the right direction (Jee Young, 2011). EI competencies and leadership strategies must be developed, learned and mastered by 21st-century leaders whether in for-profit or nonprofit organizations. Studies indicated that even leaders in the for-profit industry who benefited from extensive EI research and training are still not fully aware of what the construct is all about. According to Ingram and Cagemi (2012), the real meaning behind feelings is still not clear to some people; some people are still associating typical emotional responses such sadness and happiness to emotions. Ingram and Cagemi (2012) added that an EI leader look beyond mere feelings but demonstrated awareness of personal feelings ahead of their impact on the subordinates. The leader's ability to recognize his or her emotions and that of their subjects simultaneously is what make such a leader an EI leader (Iuscu et al., 2012).

Understanding the intricacies surrounding what constituted EI skills require a training program geared toward harnessing these skills. The marked differences in motives of establishment between the nonprofit and their for-profit counterpart called for a sector-based or context-based training that will meet the unique need of the nonprofit leaders. It could be recalled that the lack of identity, the not for profit status, and the withdrawal of government financial supports recently drifted the NPOs to start adopting the for-profit management style (Lindenberg, 2001). According to Keller (2011), the rate of NPOs' replication of the for-profit management techniques is alarming. The incessant desires of the nonprofit leaders to seek the top-of-the-line management training like their for-profit counterpart is a clear indication of an identity crisis (Keller, 2011).

A context-based training program with input from EI curriculum for the purpose of the improving the leadership of this sector can make sense. Adopting context-based training programs is better than putting a square peg in a round hole in the name of copying the approach that works (Bunchapattanasakda et al., 2012). According to Krishnaveni and Deepa (2011), practitioners of leadership are rigorously engaging EI training programs to improve leadership strategies.

This qualitative descriptive study has many contributions to the body of knowledge in the sense that it may be the first research that examines the nonprofit leaders' perceptions about the value of EI on leadership strategies. Several research studies are found about EI and for-profit leadership. This research also contributed to the body of knowledge by showcasing the feasibility of using qualitative research method in the study. Several studies with a related topic are predominantly conducted using the quantitative method and correlational designs. The plethora of studies linking EI to leadership effectiveness in other sectors made a similar study with NPO leaders a topic of interest (Bhullar, Schutte, & Malouf, 2012).

References

Abdul, L., & Ehiobuche, C. (2011). *Emotional intelligence and managerial competence. Insights to a Changing World, 2011(4),* 41-54. Retrieved from http://www.franklinpublishing.net.

Adeoye, H., & Torubelli, V. (2011). Emotional intelligence and human relationship managers as predictors of organizational commitment. *IFE Psychologia, 19* (2), 212-226

Akins, L. J. (2015). *Relationship between emotional intelligence in Black leaders of XYZ church and their employee's job satisfaction.* (Doctoral Dissertation). Retrieved from Dissertation and Theses@ University of Phoenix, UMI: 370739

Allio, R. (2013). Leaders and leadership-many theories, but what advice is reliable. *Strategy & Leadership, 41*(1), 4-14. doi.10:1108/10878571311290016

Amiri, M. P., Amiri, M. P., & Amiri, A. P. (2010). A dynamic model of contingency leadership effectiveness. *Clinical Leadership*

& *Management Review, 24* (2), 1-10. Retrieved from search.ebscohost.com.

Armitage, A., & Keeble-Allen, D. (2008). Undertaking a structured literature review or structuring a literature review: Tales from the field. *Electronic Journal of Business Research Methods, 6* (2), 103-113. Retrieved from www.ejbm.com

Arbnor, I., & Bjerke, B. (2009). *Methodology for creating business knowledge (3rd ed.)*.Stockholm, Sweden: Sage.

Artherton, A., & Elmore, R. (2007). Structuring qualitative enquiry in management and organization research: A dialogue on the merits of using software for qualitative data analysis: Qualitative Research in Organizations and Management. *An International Journal, 2* (1), 62-77. doi: 10:1108/17465640710749117

Ashkanasy, N. M., & Dashborough, M. T. (2003). Emotional awareness and emotional intelligence in leadership teaching. *Journal of Education for Business, 79* (1), 18-22, http://dx.doi.org/10:1080/08832320309599082

Austin-Roberson, K. (2009). Making better, stronger churches through organizational design. *Journal of Strategic Leadership, 2* (1), 27-39. Retrieved from www.regent.edu/acad/global/publications/.../home.htm

Bar-On, R. (1997). Bar-On Emotional Quotient Inventory (EQ-i): *Technical manual. Toronto: Multi-Health System.* Retrieved from www.eiconsortium.org/measures/eqi.htm

Batool, B. (2013). Emotional intelligence and effective leadership. *Journal of Business Studies Quarterly, 4* (3), 84-94. Retrieved from jbsq.org

Baxter, P., & Jack, S. (2008). Qualitative case study methodology: Study design and implementation for novice researchers. *The Qualitative Report, 13*(4), 544-559. Retrieved from www.nova.edu/ssss/QR/QR13.../baxter.pdf

Bernard, R.H. (2012). *Social research methods: Qualitative and quantitative approaches (2nd ed.).* Thousand Oaks, CA: Sage.

Bhullar, N., Schutte, N.S., & Malouff, J.M. (2012). Traits emotional intelligence as a moderator of the relationship between psychological distress and satisfaction with life. *Individual Differences Research, 10* (1), 19-26

Bono, J., & Anderson, M. (2005). The advice and influence networks of transformational leaders. *Journal of Applied Psychology, 90* (6), 1306-1314. doi.10:1037/0021-9010.90.6.1306.

Borrego, M., Douglas, E.P., & Amelink, C.T. (2009). Quantitative, qualitative, and mixed methods in engineering education. *Journal of Engineering Education, 98*(1), 53-66. doi: 10.1002/j.2168-9830.2009.tb01005.x

Bottomley, K., Burgess, S., & Fox, M. (2014). Are the behaviors of transformational leaders impacting organizations: A study of transformational leadership. *International Management Review, 10* (1), 5-9. Retrieved from connection.ebscohost.com

Bryman, A., & Bell, E. (2015). *Business research methods (2nd ed.).* New York, NY: Oxford Press.

Bruce, D., Deskins, J. A., Hill, B. C., & Rork, J. C. (2007). Small business and state growth: An econometric investigation. *SBA Office of Advocacy Research Report.* SBAHQ-05-M-0410. Retrieved from researchgate.net

Bunchapattanasakda, C., Wiriyakosol, S., & Ya-anan, M. (2012). Leadership roles on employees retaining practice in nonprofit organization: *The case of Thailand. International Journal of Business and Social Science, 3*(8), 1-22. Retrieved from ijbssnet.com.

Buys, C., & Rothman, S. (2010). Burnout and engagement of reformed church ministers. *South African Journal of Industrial Psychology, 36* (1), 1-11. Retrieved from www. Sajip.com

Cepeda, G., & Martin, D. (2005). A review of case studies publishing in Management Decision 2003-2004: Guides and criteria for achieving quality in qualitative research. *Management Decision, 43* (5/6), 851-876.

http://dx.doi.org/10.1108/00251740510603600

Chan, Z. C., & Cheuk, W. (2009). A descriptive study on adolescents' experiences of using ICQ (seek you). *The qualitative report, 14*(1), 1-19. Retrieved from

http://www.nova.edu/ssss/QR/QR14-1/chan.pdf

Cherniss, C. (2010). Emotional intelligence: Toward clarification of a concept. *Industrial and Organizational Psychology, 32*(2) 110-126, doi.10.1111/j.1754-9434.2010.01231.x

Cheverton, J. (2007). Holding our own: Effect and performance in nonprofit organizations. *Australian Journal of Social Issues, 42*(2), 427-436. Retrieved http://search.informit.com.au/documentSummary;dn=926672966331564;res=IELHSS> ISSN: 0157-6321

Chopra, P.K., & Kanji, G.K. (2010). Emotional intelligence: A catalyst for inspirational leadership and management excellence. *Total Quality Management & Business Excellence, 21*(10), 971-1004. http://dx.doi.org/10.1080/14783363.2010.487704

Chowdhury, I. A. (2015). Issue of quality in a qualitative research: An overview. *Innovative Issues and Approaches in Social Science, 8* (1), 142-162. http://dx.doi.org/10.12959/issn.1855-0541.IIASS-2015-no1-art09

Christensen, L. B., Johnson, R. B., & Turner, L. A. (2011). *Research methods, design, and analysis (11 ed)*. Boston, MA: Allyn & Bacon

Colfax, R. S., Rivera, J. J., & Perez, K. T. (2010). Applying emotional intelligence, (EQ-I) in the workplace: Vital to global business success. *Journal of International Business Research 9* (1), 89-98. Retrieved from www.questia.com.

Creswell, J. W. (2013). *Qualitative inquiry & research design: Choosing among five approaches. (2nd ed.)*. Thousand Oaks, CA: Sage

Creswell, J. W. (2012). Research design: *Qualitative, quantitative, and mixed methods approaches. (2nd ed.)*. Thousand Oaks, CA: Sage

Crowe, S., Creswell, K., Robertson, A., Huby, G., Avery, A., & Sheikh, A. (2011). *The case study approach. BMC Medical Research Methodology, 11*(27), 100-115. Retrieved from www.biomedcentral.com/1471-2288/11/100

Davis, B. R., & Mentzer, J. T. (2006). Logistics service driven loyalty: A descriptive study. *Journal of Business Logistics 27* (2) , 53-67. http://dx.doi.org/10.1002/j.2158-1592.2006.tb00217.x

De Kluyver, C. A., & Pearce, J. A. (2012). *Strategy: A view from the top (4th ed.)*.Upper Saddle River, NJ: Pearson

Denzin, N., & Lincoln, Y. (2011). *The sage handbook of qualitative research (4th. Ed.)*. Thousand Oaks, CA: Sage.

Derue, D., Nahrgang, J.D., Wellman, N., & Humphrey, S.E.(2011). Trait and behavioral theories of leadership: An integration and meta-analytic test of their relative validity. *Personality Psychology, 64* (1), 7-25. doi: 10.1111/j.1744-6570.2010.01201

De Weed-Nederhof, P. C. (2001). Qualitative case study research: The case of a PhD research project on organizing and managing new product development systems. *Management Decision, 39* (7), 513-538. doi: 10.1108/EUM0000000005805

DiMiggio, P. J., Weiss, J. A., & Clotfelter, C. T. (2002). Part 1: Resources for research on selected types of nonprofit organization: Data to support scholarship on nonprofit organizations an introduction. *The American Behavioral Scientists 45*(10), 1474-1492. http://dx.doi.org/10.1177/0002764202045011003

Dolev, N., & Leshem, S. (2016). Teachers' emotional intelligence: The impact of training. *International Journal of Emotional Education.8* (1), 75-94

Dulewicz, V., & Higgs, M. (2003). Leadership at the top: The need for emotional intelligence in organization. I*nternational Journal of Organizational Analysis, 11*(3), 193-210, doi.10:1108/eb028971

Dusick, D.M. (2011). Bold educational software: Writing the theoretical framework.Retrieved from http://bold-ed.com/framework.htm

Estelle, C., Beth, F., & Lynn, M. (2013). Developing emotional intelligence ability in oncology nurses: *A clinical rounds approach. Oncology Nursing Forum, 40* (1), 22-29. http://dx.doi.org/10.1188/13.onf.22-29

Faugier, J. & Woolnough, H. (2002). *National nursing leadership program. Learning Disability Practice, 5* (10), 32-37. http://dx.doi.org/10.7748/ldp2002.12.5.10.32.c1473

Forbes Insights (2012). *Intelligence is overrated: What you really need to succeed* [Contributed by Keld Jensen]. Retrieved from http://www.forbes.com

Fusch, P. I., & Ness, L.R. (2015). Are we there yet? Data saturation in qualitative Research. *The Qualitative Report 20* (9), 1408-1416. Retrieved from http://www.nova.edu/ssss/QR/QR20/fusch1.pdf

Garcia, E.O. (2015). *The relationship between conflict management, emotional intelligence, leadership and quality in higher education.* (Doctoral Dissertation). Retrieved from Dissertation and Theses @ University of Phoenix, UMI Number:

3710742

Gardner, H. (2011). *Frames of mind: The theory of multiple intelligences.* New York, NY: Basic Books.

George, R., Goethals, S.T., Allison, R.M., & David, M.M. (2014). Conceptions of Leadership: Enduring ideas and emerging insights. *Business & Management Collections (2015), Series: Jepson Studies in Leadership.* doi 10.1057/9781137472038preview

Ghauri, P., & Gronhaug, K. (2005). *Research methods in business studies: A practical guide (3rd ed.).* London: Financial Times, Prentice Hall

Gibelman, M., & Gelman, S.R. (2001). Very public scandals: NGO in trouble. *International Society for Third-Sector Research, 2* (2), 1-15. Retrieved from link.springer.com/.../10.1023%2FA%3...

Gignac, G. (2010). Seven-factor model of emotional intelligence as measured by Genos EI: A confirmatory factor analytic investigation based on self-and rater-report data. *European Journal of Psychological Assessment, 26*(4), 309-316. http://dx.doi.org/10.1027/1015-5759/a00004

Glaser, J., & Landel, G. (2013). Life with and without coding: Two methods for early- stage data analysis in qualitative research aiming at causal explanation forum. *Qualitative Social Research, 14* (2), 1-38. Retrieved from www.qualitative- research.net.

Goh, S., & Low, B. (2014). The influence of servant leadership towards organizational commitment: The mediating role of trust in leaders. *International Journal of Business & Management, 9* (1), 17-20. http://dx.doi.org/10.5539/ijbm.v9n1p17.

Goleman, D. (1998). *Working with emotional intelligence.* London: Bloomsbury

Goleman, D. (2004). *Emotional intelligence & working with emotional intelligence.* London: Bloomsbury.

Goleman, D. (2004). What makes a leader? *Harvard Business R view,* 1-12. Retrieved from www.hbr.org

Goleman, D., Boyatzis, R., & Mckee, A. (2013). *Primal leadership: Unleashing the power of emotional intelligence.* Boston, MA: Harvard Business Review Press.

Granot, E., Bashear, T.G., & Motta, P.C. (2012). A structural guide to in-depth interviewing in business and industrial marketing research. *The Journal of Business and Industrial Marketing, 27*(7), 547-553. doi: 0.1108/08858621211257310

Grandy, G. (2013). An descriptive study of strategic leadership in churches. *Leadership & Organization Development Journal, 34* (7), 616-638. http://dx.doi.org/10.1108/lodg-08-2011-0081

Guteng, S.I. (2005). Professional concerns of beginning teachers of deaf and hard of hearing students. *American Annals of the Deaf, 150* (1), 17-41. DOI: http://dx.doi.org/10.1353/aad.2005.0018

Hahn, R., Sabou, S., Toader, R., & Radulescu, C. (2012). About emotional intelligence Leadership. *Annals of the University of Oradea, Economics Science Series, 12* (2), 744-749

Hamlin, R. (2005). Toward universalistic models of managerial effectiveness: A comparative study of recent British and American derived models of leadership. *Human Resource Development International, 8* (1), 5-25. http://dx.doi.org/10.1080/1367886042000338254

Harmer, B. M. (2006). At cross purposes: Head-to head professionalism in not-for-profit pastoral organizations. *Journal of Health Organization and Management, 20* (6), 489-501. http://dx.doi.org/10.1108/14777260610702244

Hay Group. (2011). *Emotional and social competency inventory (ESCI): A user guide for accredited practitioners.* Boston, MA: Author. Retrieved from www.haygroup.co

Hess, J. D., & Bacigalupo, A. C. (2011). Enhancing decisions and decision-making processes through the application of emotional intelligence skills. *Management Decision, 49* (5), 710-721. doi: 10:1108/10748121011072672

Hickman, G.R. (2010). *Leading organizations: Perspectives for a new era, (2nd,).* Thousand Oaks, CA: Sage Publications.

Hsieh, Y., & Chen, H. M. (2011). Strategic fit among business competitive strategy, human resource strategy, and reward system. *Academy of Strategic Management, 10* (2), 11-32

Ingram, J., & Cangemi, J. (2012). Emotions, emotional intelligence and leadership: A brief, pragmatic perspective. *Education, 132* (4), 771-778. Retrieved www. connection.ebscohost.com.

Iuscu, S., Neagu, C., & Neagu, L. (2012). Emotional intelligence essential component of leadership. *Global Conference on Business & Finance Proceedings, 7* (2), 21

Ivankova, N. V., Creswell, J. W., & Stick, S. L. (2006). Using mixed-methods sequential explanatory design: From theory to practice. F*ield Methods, 18* (1), 3-20. doi.1177/1525822x05282260

Ives Tay Assoc CIPD BBA. (2014). To what extent should data saturation be used as a quality criterion in qualitative research? *LinkedIn Pulse.* Retrieved from www.linkedin.com

Jee Young, S. (2011). The effect of high performance work systems, entrepreneurship and organizational culture on organizational performance. *Seoul Journal of Business, 17* (1), 3-16.

Jimenez, M. (2016). *A quantitative study: The relationship between managers' emotional intelligence awareness and demographics and leadership styles.* (Doctoral Dissertation). Retrieved

from Dissertation and Theses@ University of Phoenix. Pro-
Quest Number:10076471.

Joseph, D. L., & Newman, D. A. (2010). Emotional intelligence:
An integrative meta-Analysis and cascading model. *Journal of
Applied Psychology, 95* (1), 54-78. doi.10.1037/a0017286

Judge, T.A., & Bono, J.E. (2000). Five-factor model of personality
and transformational leadership. *Journal of Applied Psychology, 85* (5), 751-765. http://dx.doi.org/10.1037/0021-
9010.85.5.751

Keller, G. F. (2011). Comparing the effect of management practices
on organizational performance between for-profit and not-for-
profit corporations in the Southeast Wisconsin. *Journal of
Business and Economics Research, 9* (3), 29-37. Retrieved
from http://journals.cluteonline.com/index.PhP/JBER

Kenzer, R.C. (2001). American city, southern place: A cultural history of antebellum Richmond. *Journal of Early Republic, 21*
(1), 362-365. Retrieved from
http://dx.doi.org/10.2307/3125227

Kerr, C. (2010). Assessing and demonstrating data saturation in
qualitative inquiry supporting patient-reported outcomes research. *Expert Review of Pharmacoenonomics & Outcomes
Research,* 269-281. doi:10.1586/erp.10.30

Keung, E. K., & Rockinson-Szapkiw, A. J. (2013). The relationship
between transformational leadership and cultural intelligence:
A study of international school leaders. *Journal of Educational Administration, 51*(6), 836-854.
http://dx.doi.org/10.1108/jea-04-2012-0049.

Khalili, A. (2013). The role of emotional intelligence in work place:
A literature review. International *Journal of Management, 29*
(3), 355-370. Retrieved from www.eiconsortium.org/mem-
bers/khalili.html

Kramer, K., & Nayak, P. (2013). *A plan A: How successful nonprofits develop their future leaders. Boston, MA: The Bridgespan Group.* Retrieved from http://www.bridgespan.org/getattachment/6c85916-adb 1-43dd-a3b8-2ddbb238cfa2/Plan-A-How-succcesful-Nonprofits-Develop-Leades.aspx

Krell, E. (2013). Exploring what it takes to lead in 21st century: The continuous strategic planning and other leadership competencies. *Baylor Business, 31*(2), 5-8. Retrieved from www.bbr.baylor.edu/exploring-leadership

Krishnaveni, R. R. & Deepa, R.R. (2011). Emotional intelligence: A soft tool for competitive advantage in the organizational context. *IUP Journal Skills, 5* (2), 51-62. Retrieved from www. connection.ebscohost.com.

Kurland, H., Peretz, H., & Hertz, L. (2010). Leadership style and organizational learning: The immediate effect of school vision. Journal of Educational Administration, 48 (1), 7-30. doi: 10:1108/09578231011015395

Lambert, V.A., & Lambert, C.E. (2012). Qualitative descriptive research: An acceptable design. *Pacific Rim International Journal of Nursing Research, 16* (4), 255-256

Laub, J. D. (2010-2011). Leadership: It's not just a challenge, it's an adventure. *National Forum of Educational Administration and Supervision Journal, 27* (2), 43-49. Retrieved from www.slideshare.net.

Larin, H. M., Benson, G., Wessel, J., & Williams, R. (2011). Examining change in emotional social intelligence, caring, and leadership in health professional students. *Journal of Allied Health, 40* (20), 96-102. Retrieved from www.ncbi.nlm.nih.gov.

Law, K. S, Wong, C., & Song, L. J. (2004). The construct and criterion validity of emotional intelligence and its potential utility for management studies. *Journal of Applied Psychology, 89* (3), 483-496. http://dx.doi.org/10.1037/0021-9010.89.3.483

Leedy, P. D., & Ormrod, J. E. (2009. *Practical research: Planning and design (9th ed.).* Upper Saddle River, NJ: Prentice Hall

Leech, N. L., & Onwuegbuzie, A. J. (2011). Beyond constant comparison qualitative data analysis: Using NVivo. *School Psychology, 26* (1), 70-84. doi: 10.1037/a0022711

Lecy, J. D., Schitz, H. P., & Swedland, H. (2012). Non-governmental and not-for-profit organizational effectiveness. *Third-Sector Research, 2012* (23), 434-451. http://dx.doi.org/10.1007/s11266-011-9204-6

Lincoln, Y. S., & Guba, E. G. (1985). *Naturalistic Inquiry.* Newbury Park, California: Sage Publications Inc.

Lindenberg, M. (2001). Are we at the cutting edge or the blunt edge: Improving NGO organizational performance with private and public sector. *Strategic Managements Frameworks, 11*(3), 247-270. http://dx.doi.org/10.1002/nml.11302

Magilvy, J. K., & Thomas, E. (2009). A first qualitative project: Qualitative descriptive design for novice researchers. *Journal for Specialists in Pediatric Nursing, 14* (4), 298-300. doi:10.1111/!.1777-6155.2009.00212.x

Manolis, J. C., Chan, K. M., Finkelstein, M. E., Stephens, S., Nelson, C. R., Grant, J. B., & Dombeck, M. P. (2009). *Leadership: A new frontier in conservative science. Conservation Biology, 23*(4), 879-886. http://dx.doi.org/10.1111/j.1523-1739.2008.01150.x

Marshall, B., Cardon, P., Poddar, A., & Fontenot, R. (2013). Does sample size matter in qualitative research?: A review of qualitative interviews in is research. *Journal of Computer Information Systems, 54*(1), 11-22. Retrieved from iacis.org/jcis/articles/JCIS54-2.pdf

Mason, M. (2010). Sample size and saturation in PhD studies using qualitative interviews. *Forum: Qualitative Social Research, 11*(3), 1-20. Retrieved from www.qualitative-research.net › Home › Vol 11, No 3 (2010)

Mayer, J. D., Salovey, P., & Caruso, D. (2002). *The Mayer-Salovey-Caruso emotional intelligence test (MSCEIT), version 2.0.* Toronto, Canada: Multi Health System

McKenzie, G., Runte, M., Usher, J., & Runte, R. (2013). The impact of neo-conservatism on the charitable sector: Nonprofit to nonprofit? *Journal of American Academy of Business, 19* (1), 181-190

McMurray, A. J., Pirola-Merlo, A., Sarros, J. C., & Islam, M. M. (2010). Leadership, climate, psychological capital, commitment, and well-being in nonprofit organization. *Leadership & Organizational Development Journal, 31*(5), 436-457. doi: 10.1108/01437731011056452

MentalHelp.net. (2016). *The big five personality traits.* Retrieved from http://www.mentalhelp.net

Merriam, S. (2009). *Case study research in education: A qualitative approach.* San Francisco, CA: Jossey-Bass.

Meyer, C. K., & Taylor, A. (2013). Nonprofit and public sector human resources management. *International Journal of Management & Information Systems, 17*(3), 135-162.

Michel, A., Stegmaier, R., & Sonntag, K. (2010). I scratch your back-you scratch mine: Do procedural justice and organizational identification matter for employees' cooperation during change? *Journal of Change Managers, 10* (1), 41-59. http://dx.doi.org/10.1080/14697010903549432

Neera, J., Anjanee, S., & Shoma, M. (2010). Leadership dimensions and challenges in the new millennium. *Advances in Management, 3* (3), 18-24. Retrieved from www. connection.ebscohost.com/.../leadership-dimensions-challenges-new-mill...

Neuman, W. L. (2009). *Social research methods: Quantitative and qualitative approaches (7th e.d)*. Boston, MA: Pearson Education

Qualitative Research Methods: (2015). *A data collector's field guide. Northeastern University College of Computer and Information Technology.* Retrieved June, 2015 from www.ccs.neu.edu

QSR International. (2015). *NVivo10 tutorials.* Retrieved from http://www.qsrinternational.com

Oliver, G. (2004). Investigating information cultures: A comparative case study research design and methods. *Archival Science, 2004* (4), 287-317. http://dx.doi.org/10.1007/s10502-005-2596-6

Olson, B., Parayitam, S., Pinos, V., & Twigg, N. (2006). Leadership in the 21 century: *The value of emotional intelligence. Academy of Strategic Management Journal, 5* (5), 61-76.

Onwuegbuzie, A.J., & Collins, K.M. (2010). A typology of mixed methods sampling designs in social science research. The *Qualitative Report, 12* (2), 281-316. http://www.nova.edu.sss/QR/QR12-2/onwuegbuzie2.pdf.

O'Reilly, M. & Parker, N. (2012). Unsatisfactory Saturation: A critical exploration of the notion of saturated sample size in qualitative research. *Qualitative Research Journal,* 1-8. doi.10.1177/1468794112446106

Otaroghene, P. (2012). Situational and contingency theories of leadership: Are they the same. *IOSR Journal of Business and Management (IOSR), 4*(3), 13-17. www.iosrjournals.org.

Parris, D., & Peachey, J. (2013). A systematic literature review of servant leadership theory in organizational context. *Springer Science + Business Media, 22* (1), 377-399. doi:

10.1007/310551-012-1322-6.

Patton, M. Q. (1990). *Qualitative evaluation and research methods (2nd ed.)*. Newbury Park, CA: Sage Publications.

Ployhart, R. E., Lim, B., & Chan, K (2001). Exploring relations between typical and maximum performance ratings and the five factor model of personality. *Personnel Psychology, 54* (4), 809-843. doi: 10.1111/j.1744-6570.2001.tb00233.x

Polychroniou, P. V. (2009). Relationship between emotional intelligence and transformational leadership of supervisors: The impact on team effectiveness. *Team Performance Management, 15* (7/8), 343-356.
http://dx.doi.org/10.1108/13527590911002122

Prandini, M., Isler, P.V., Barthelmess, P. (2012). Responsible management education for 21-century leadership. *Central European Business Review, 1*(2), 16-22).
http://dx.doi.org/10.18267/j.cebr.13

Purpose of Research: *Exploratory, Descriptive & Explanatory- Video & Lesson* (2015). Retrieved from:
http://study.com/academy/lesson/purposes-of-research-exploratory-descriptive.html

Rajah, R., Song, Z., & Arvey, R. D. (2011). Emotionality and leadership. Taking stock of the past decade of research. T*he Leadership Quarterly, 22* (6), 1107-1119.
http://dx.doi.org/10.1016/j.leaqua.2011.09.006

Ramesh, V. S. (2013), Emotional intelligence in leadership: A conceptual review. International *Journal of Organizational Behavior & Management Perspectives, 2* (1), 210-216.

Riggio, R. E., & Reichard, R. (2008). The emotional and social intelligence of effective leadership: *An emotional and social skill approach. Journal of Managerial Psychology, 23*(2), 169-185. http://dx.doi.org/10.1108/02683940810850808

Rosenzweig, P. (2007). By invitation: The halo value, and other managerial delusions. *McKinsey Quarterly, 1*(1), 76-85. Retrieved from www.mckinsey.com

Ross, N. (2012). Epoch of transformation: An interpersonal leadership model for the 21st century part1. *Integral Leadership Review, 12* (1), 1-20. Retrieved from integralleadershipreview.com

Rothman, S., & Buys, C. (2011). Job demands and resources, psychological conditions, religious coping and work engagement of reformed church. *Journal of Psychology in Africa, 21*(2), 173-183. doi: 10.1080/14330237.2011.10820446

Routio, P. (2007). *Sampling.* Retrieved from http://www.uiah.fi/projekti/metodi/152.htm.

Sadri, G. (2012). Emotional intelligence and leadership development. *Public Personnel Management, 41*(3), 535-544. http://dx.doi.org/10.1177/009102601204100308

Safferstone, M. J. (2005).Organizational leadership: Classic works and contemporary perspectives. *Choice, 42*(6), 959-975. Retrieved from ProQuest Central

Sakiru, O. K., Enoho, D. V., Kareem, S. D., & Abdullahi, M. (2013). Relationship between employee performance, leadership styles and emotional intelligence in an organization. IOSR, *Journal of Humanities and Social Science, 8* (2), 53-57. Retrieved from www.iosrjournal.org. http://dx.doi.org/10.9790/0837-0825357

Salamon, L. M., & Helmut, K. A. (1997). *Defining the nonprofit sector: A Cross-national analysis, (John Hopkins Nonprofit Sector Series),* New York, NY: Manchester University Press

Saliu, S.K. (2013). A descriptive inquiry into psychological biases in financial investment behavior. *The Journal of Behavioral Finance, 14* (2013), 94-103. doi:10.1080/1542756-

2013.790387

Salamon, L. M. (1999). The nonprofit sector at crossroads: The case of America. *International Journal of Voluntary and Non-profit Organizations, 10* (1), 1-22. Retrieved from www.link.springer.com

Sandelowski, M. (2000). Focus on research methods: Whatever happened to qualitative descriptions? *Research in Nursing & Health,* Retrieved from http:www.wou.edu/-mcgladm/Qualita-tive%20methods/optional%20stuff/qualitative%20descrip-tion.pd

Saxena, S. (2014). Are transformational leaders creative and cre-ative leaders transformational: An attempted synthesis through the big five factor model of personality lens. *Aweshkar Re-search Journal, 18*(2), 30-51

Schwandt, T.A. (2015). *The sage dictionary of qualitative inquiry.* Thousand Oaks, CA: Sage Publications Inc.

Schoenhaus, R. M. (2002). The training for peace and humanitarian relief operations: Advancing best practice. *Peace works, 2002*(43), 1-43. Retrieved from: www.usip.org.

Seidman, I. (2013). *Interviewing as qualitative research: A guide for researchers in education & social sciences (4th ed.).* New York, NY: Teachers College

Sendjaya, S. (2015). Personal and organizational excellence through servant leadership: Learning to serve, serving to lead, leading to transform. *Management for Professional Series. Springer International Publishing Switzerland 2015.* Re-trieved from http://dx.doi.org/ 10.1007/978-3-319-16196-9_9

Shahhossein, M., Silong, A., Ismaill, I., & Uli, J. (2012). The role of EI on job performance. *International Journal of Business and Social Science, 3*(21), 1-7.
Retrieved from www.ijbsset.com.

Shenton, A. (2004). Strategies for ensuring trustworthiness in qualitative research projects. *Education for Information*, 22, 63-75

Sims-Vanzant, C. (2007), *Emotional intelligence and leadership
practices among human service program managers.* (Doctoral
Dissertation), UMI Number: 3265690. Retrieved from Pro-
Quest Digital Dissertation Database.

Singleton, R. A., & Straits, B. C. (2009). *Approaches to social research (5th e.d).* New York, NY: Oxford University Press.

Snodgrass, L.D. (2015). *Phenomenological study on healthcare
workers' perceptions of employee engagement servant leadership and emotional intelligence.* (Doctoral Dissertation). Retrieved from Dissertation and Theses @University of Phoenix,
UMI Number: 10065217

Stevens, W. (2010). *Using emotional intelligence as a leadership
strategy to make good leaders great.* (Doctoral Dissertation)
UMI No. 3569338. Retrieved from ProQuest Dissertation
Database

Swanson, Andree, Bowler, Brand, Zobisch, and Paula (2014). An
assessment of emotional intelligence understanding in the
field of real estate. *Institute for Business & Finance Research,*
9(2), 43-51. Retrieved from search.proquest.com

Sword, W., Heaman, M., Brook, S., Tough, S., & Patricia, A.
(2012). Women's and care providers perspectives of quality
prenatal care: A qualitative descriptive study. *BMC   Preg-
nancy and Childbirth, 12*(29), 1-18.
http://dx.doi.org/10.1186/1471-2393-12-29

Theodoridis, C. (2014). A phenomenological case study: Strategy
development in small And medium retail enterprises in Greece
during recession. *Sage Research Methods Cases.* DOI:
http://dx.doi.org./10.4135/978144627305014539099.

Thomas, E. & Magilvy, J. K. (2011). Qualitative Rigor or Research

Validity in Qualitative Research. *Journal for Specialists in Pediatric Nursing, 16*, 151-155. http://dx.doi.org/10.1111/j.1744-6155.2011.00283.x

Trautmann, K., Maher, J. K., & Motley, D. G. (2007). Learning strategies as predictors for transformational leadership: The case of nonprofit managers. *Leadership & Organizational Development Journal, 28*(3), 269-287. http://dx.doi.org/10.1108/01437730710739675.

Tucker, M.L, Sojka, J.Z., Barone, F.J., & McCarthy, A.M. (2000). Training Tomorrow's

Leaders: Enhancing the Emotional Intelligence of Business Graduates. *Journal of Education for Business, 6*(75), 331-337 doi: 10.1080/08832320009599036

Urban Institute (2012). *Research areas: Nonprofit sector.* Retrievefrom http://www.urban.org/nonprofits/more.cfm

Venkatesh, J., & Balaji, M. (2012). The contribution of emotional intelligence to MBA students by imbibing better leaders' behavior. *Indian Stream Research Journal, 1* (12), 1-4. Retrieved from www.isrj.org/ArchiveArticle.aspx?ArticleID=615

Walker, J.L. (2012). The use of saturation in qualitative research. Canadian *Journal of Cardiovascular Nusing, 22*(2), 37-46. Retrieved from http://www.cccn.ca

Wong, S.S., & NG, V. (2008). A qualitative and quantitative study of psychotherapists congruence in Singapore. *Psychotherapy Research, 18*(1), 58-76. doi:10.1080/10503300-701324654

Wren, J. (2013). *The leader's companion: Insights on leadership through the ages.* New York, NY: The Free Press.

Yin, R. K.(2003a). *Multi-case study research: Design and methods (3rd.).* Thousand Oaks, CA: Sage Publication.

Yin, R. K. (2011). Application of case study research. (2nd e.d.). Thousand Oaks, CA: Sage Publications

Yin, R. K. (2015). *Case study research: Design & methods (5th e.d.).* Thousand Oaks, CA: Sage Publications Inc.

Zopiatis, A., Constanti, P. (2010). Leadership styles and burnout: Is there an association. *International Journal of Contemporary Hospitality Management,* 22(3), 300-320. DOI: 10.1108/0959611101103592

Appendix A
Informed Consent

INFORMED CONSENT: PARTICIPANTS 18 YEARS OF AGE AND OLDER

Dear Participant:

My name is

      I am conducting a research study titled, A DESCRIPTIVE INQUIRY INTO THE NONPROFIT LEADERS' PERCEPTIONS OF THE VALUE OF EMOTIONAL INTELLIGENC ON LEADERSHIP. The purpose of this research is to explore the perceptions of NPO leaders about the value of EI on leadership strategies in the City of Richmond, Virginia. This qualitative study will adopt Seidman's three phase interviews process to explore the experiences of NPO leaders. The first phase of the Seidman's interview phases will explore the context of the study. The second phase will explore the professional experiences of participants. The third phase will be used to review the interview script with the participants. Fourteen participants will be selected and subjected to in-depth face-to-face interviews (in person or Skype), or through the phone depending on the participant's preference.

      Your participation will involve taking part in the preselection interviews. If you are selected to participate in the study, you will be required to take part in the in-depth interview sessions which may last for 55-60 minutes each. You can decide to be a part of this study or not. Once you start, you can withdraw from the study at any time without any penalty or loss of benefits. The results of the research study may be published but your identity will remain confidential and your name will not be made known to any outside party.

In this research, there are no foreseeable risks to you "none"

Although there may be no direct benefit to you, a possible benefit from your being part of this study is you will have the opportunity to contribute to the leadership development of nonprofit sector. This study may also help you consider knowing your emotional intelligence level.

For questions about your rights as a study participant, or any concerns or complaints, please contact the University of Phoenix Institutional Review Board via email at IRB@phoenix.edu.

As a participant in this study, you should understand the following:

1. You may decide not to be part of this study or you may want to withdraw from the study at any time. If you want to withdraw, you can do so without any problems.

2. Your identity will be kept confidential.

3. Emmanuel Peter, the researcher, has fully explained the nature of the research study and has answered all of your questions and concerns.

4. If interviews are done, they may be recorded. If they are recorded, you must give permission for the researcher, Emmanuel Peter, to record the interviews. You understand that the information from the recorded interviews may be transcribed. The researcher will develop a way to code the data to ensure that your name is protected.

5. Data will be kept in a secure and locked area. The data will be kept for three years, and then destroyed.

6. The results of this study may be published.

"By signing this form, you agree that you understand the nature of the study, the possible risks to you as a participant, and how your identity will be kept confidential. When you sign this form, this means that you are 18 years old or older and that you give your permission to volunteer as a participant in the study that is described here."

(0) **I accept the above terms.**   (0) **I do not accept the above terms**.
(CHECK ONE)

Signature of the interviewee _____

Date _____

Signature of the researcher:

Appendix B
Interview Questions

The following are sample interview questions drafted for this study. These interview questions are designed to meet Seidman's three phase interview process. Based on Seidman's interview process, the first phase is set aside for the pre-screening of the study participants. The second phase is set aside for the exploration of detailed professional experiences of the participants. Finally, the third phase is set aside for the review of the interview script before data analysis (Seidman, 2013).

Seidman's phase one questions (Context of the study/prescreening interviews).

1. May I know your position in your organization? Or are you in any executive position?
2. How do you categorize your organization? Or do you consider your organization a NPOs?
3. What level of education have you attended? Or are you a four year college graduate?
4. Please tell me how long you have been in this position? Or, have you been in this position for at least three years?
5. In this position, how many employee do you have under your supervision? If it is a religious organization, how many member do you have while in this position?
6. What is emotional intelligence to you?

Seidman's phase two interview questions (Participant Professional Experiences)

1. Given the delicate nature of leadership duties in the 21st-century, how would you foresee the role of emotional skills in leadership? Please explain
2. Assuming you have a stressful day at work because of workload and other inconveniences? How would you manage the stress so that you would not transfer the aggression to an innocent co-worker and what skill would you

use?

3. Supposing you encounter an annoying co-worker in your organization, how would you handle this type of person and what skill would you use?

4. Assuming you are called upon to head a high performing team in your workplace, but the team members seem unwilling to follow rules because they are experts themselves. How would you lead this type of workforce, and what skill would you use?

5. Supposing you are in a position to take a challenging leadership decision that requires the contribution of ideas, how would you collate ideas appropriately and what skill would you use?

6. Assuming EI knowledge is critical to your leadership effectiveness, how would you share the knowledge with people in your industry or people around you?

Seidman's Phase 3 interview questions (In this phase interview scripts will be played back for the participants to review, amend, and approve)

1.Do you have any final thought about your EI knowledge and leadership?

2.Please listen to your interview script and make necessary review, additions, and or subtractions.

Appendix C:
Field Test Interview Scripts

Volunteer #1

Hello my name is Emmanuel A. Peter.

. I am conducting a research that seeks to explore the perceptions of NPO leaders about the value of EI on leadership strategies.

Interviewer: I understand that you are a faculty member in the University of Phoenix, may I know how long you have been in this position?

Volunteer. 1: I have been in this position for the past 10 years.

Interviewer: That is interesting!

Interviewer: Do you happen to have people working under you, if yes, how many are they?

Volunteer 1: No, I do not have people working under me

Interviewer: What is emotional intelligence to you?

Volunteer. 1: To the best of my knowledge, emotional intelligence is the ability to study the emotions of oneself and emotions of others.

Interviewer: That is very interesting. But what do you hope to achieve by studying these emotions?

Volunteer.1: To make good leadership and relational decisions.

Interviewer: Given the delicate nature of leadership duties in the 21st-century, how would you foresee the role of EI in leadership roles? Please explain

Volunteer 1: Of course emotional skills is foreseeable in the success of 21st-century leadership. Because there is greater need to understand the people around you.

Interviewer: Assuming you have a stressful day at work because of workload and other inconveniences? How would you manage the stress so that you would not transfer the aggression to an innocent co-worker and what skill would you use?

Volunteer.1: I will look into the cause of stress and use my enduring skills to manage it

Interviewer: Supposing you encounter an annoying co-worker in your organization, how would you handle this type of person and what skill would you use?

Volunteer 1: Handling annoying person requires emotional skills and finding why the person is annoying in order to help the person and help myself.

Interviewer: Assuming you are called upon to head a high performing team in your workplace, but the team members seem unwilling to follow rules because they are experts themselves. How would you lead this type of workforce, and what skill would you use?

Volunteer 1: I will need emotional skills to lead this set of people. I will have to sit down and analyze my job knowledge vis-à-vis their expert knowledge. I will emphasize the need to achieve organization goals as important purpose of the team.

Interviewer: Supposing you are in a position to take a challenging leadership decision that requires the contribution of ideas, how would you collate ideas appropriately and what skill would you use?

Volunteer 1: First of all, I must have what I brought to the table. Secondly, I will not be bias in the analysis of ideas. What I mean here is, a good idea will be accepted irrespective of who brought it.

Interviewer: Assuming EI knowledge is critical to your leadership effectiveness, how would you share the knowledge with people in your industry or people around you?

Volunteer 1: I will simply train people about EI and its importance.

Interviewer: Now what is your final thought about EI and leadership?

Volunteer 1: I will say everybody especially people in the leadership position should have a basic knowledge of what EI is all about. The world can be a better place if everybody are aware of their emotions.

Interviewer: This is the end of the interview session. Thank you so much for your time and useful contributions. Please, before we go, can we take a few moment to review the interview script?

Volunteer #2

Hello my name is Emmanuel A. Peter.

. I am conducting a research that seeks to explore perceptions of NPO leaders about the value of EI on leadership strategies.

Interviewer: I understand that you are a faculty member in the University of Phoenix, may I know how long you have been in this position?

Volunteer.2: I have been in this position for six year now

Interviewer: How many people work under your supervision in this position?

Volunteer.2: I have no employee under my supervision

Interviewer: What is emotional intelligence to you?

Volunteer.2: To me, EI relates how I am in touch with my emotional side. EI explains how I perceive phenomenon in the world or my environment.

Interviewer: Why is getting in touch with your emotional side important to you?

Volunteer 2: It is important because it helps me to understand the day to day living and phenomenon around the world.

Interviewer: Given the delicate nature of leadership duties in the 21st-century, how would you foresee the role of EI in leadership?

Volunteer.2: I believe the very nature of good leadership traits involves some level of emotional intelligence skillsets in order to be effective as a leader.

Interviewer: Assuming you have a stressful day at work because of workload and other inconveniences? How would you manage the stress so that you would not transfer the aggression to an innocent co-worker and what skill would you use?

Volunteer.2: I would use destressing strategies I currently utilize in my current role when I've had a stressful day, exercise, breathing techniques, music or walk my dogs.

Interviewer: Supposing you encounter an annoying co-worker in your organization, how would you handle this type of person and what skill would you use?

Volunteer 2: I would exercise patience, coping skills and use a rational approach to gaining insights as to how to resolve what was making me annoyed with this particular co-worker.

Interviewer: I love your honesty, but I am talking about a situation where you come in contact with a co-worker that annoys you, but you may not have necessarily annoyed the person?

Volunteer.2: Oh you mean a co-worker that annoys me or trying to make me mad. Okay, I will need a heavy dose of emotional skills to handle this type of person.

Interviewer: Assuming you are called upon to head a high performing team in your workplace, but the team members seem unwilling to follow rules because they are experts themselves. How would you lead this type of workforce, and what skill would you use?

Volunteer.2: I would use reasoning and stern boundary skills in helping them to recognize their behavior is wrong and detrimental to them and the team and ultimately changing their behavior to a more compliant behavior as the work place code of conduct calls for.

Interviewer: Supposing you are in a position to take a challenging leadership decision that requires the contribution of ideas, how would you collate ideas appropriately and what skill would you use?

Volunteer.2: My creative skill I believe would be the most effective skillset or trait that would be useful in this particular scenario. When being asked to contribute ideas to decisions involving leadership having a creative mind helps to produce those ideas being asked for.

Interviewer: Assuming EI knowledge is critical to your leadership effectiveness, how would you share the knowledge with people in your industry or people around you?

Volunteer.2: People in the industry might be communicated to during professional interaction scenarios such as conferences, work interactions, social interactions. I would imagine I would share those traits each day with the people I work with since the very nature of our interactions would illicit situations that would call for the use of EI in many of those interactions.

Interviewer: Now what is your final thought about EI and leadership?

Volunteer 2: I will gladly recommend at least a basic EI knowledge to everyone no matter the position the person occupies.

Interviewer: This is the end of the interview session. Thank you so much for your time and useful contributions. Please, before we go, can we take a few moment to review the interview script?

Volunteer #3

Hello my name is Emmanuel A. Peter.

. I am conducting a research that seeks to explore the perceptions of NPO leaders about the value of EI on leadership strategies.

Interviewer: I understand that you are a faculty member in the University of Phoenix, may I know how long you have been in this position?

Volunteer.3: I have been in this position for five year now

Interviewer: How many people work under your supervision in this position?

Volunteer.3: I do not have any worker under my supervision

Interviewer: What is emotional intelligence to you?

Volunteer 3: EI to me is being able to understand the emotions of people around me

Interviewer: Given the delicate nature of leadership duties in the 21st-century, how would you foresee the role of EI in leadership roles? Please explain

Volunteer 3: From the look of things, EI will play important part in virtually all aspect of leadership roles.

Interviewer: Assuming you have a stressful day at work because of workload and other inconveniences? How would you manage the stress so that you would not transfer the aggression to an innocent co-worker and what skill would you use?

Volunteer 3: I will get away from the situation for moment and think and pray about it.

Interviewer: Supposing you encounter an annoying co-worker in your organization, how would you handle this type of person and what skill would you use?

Volunteer.3: I will try to consider what cause the person to act the way he did. I will take time to analyze the situation in order to arrive at the best approach to handle the situation.

Interviewer: Assuming you are called upon to head a high performing team in your workplace, but the team members seem unwilling to follow rules because they are experts themselves. How would you lead this type of workforce, and what skill would you use?

Volunteer.3: I will try to call a meeting to address all the team members about the group process. I will show video about group process and also use the opportunity to set the ground rules for the team. If these process does not work, I will present a case study of the situation to the team members to ponder over. The last resort will be to talk to them one-on-one before any disciplinary action may be taken.

Interviewer: Supposing you are in a position to take a challenging leadership decision that requires the contribution of ideas, how would you collate ideas appropriately and what skill would you use?

Volunteer.3: First of all, I must research the leadership topic under consideration adequately in order to have expert knowledge in the topic. Second, I will analyze ideas brought to table critically in order not to decide with fear or favor.

Interviewer: Assuming EI knowledge is critical to your leadership effectiveness, how would you share the knowledge with people in your industry or people around you?

Volunteer. 3: I will train people about EI. I will also organize workshops and conferences to enlighten people about EI.

Interviewer: This is the end of the interview session. Thank you so much for your time and useful contributions. Please, before we go, can we take a few moment to review the interview script?

Appendix D:
Introduction Letter to Participants

Dear xxx Leader,

My name is Emmanuel Peter, and

. I am conducting a dissertation research

This descriptive qualitative study entitled A DESCRIP-TIVE INQUIRY INTO THE NONPROFIT LEADERS' PERCEPTIONS ABOUT THE VALUE EMOTIONAL INTELLIGENCE ON LEADERSHIP will attempt to explore the perceptions of nonprofit leaders about the value of emotional intelligence on leadership strategies.

The research study offers a win-win opportunity for me the researcher and you the participant. There is no doubt that this study will assist me achieve my educational goals, but your participation will avail you of the opportunity to know more about this new form of intelligence. Studies revealed that emotional intelligence cannot be done without by any leader. Multinational companies are spending thousands of dollars to train their leaders to acquire this unique type of intelligence. The opportunity to participate in this study and the accompanied benefits is offered to you free of charge. Your participation in the study will also add you to record as one of the contributors to leadership development of nonprofit organizations.

Your participation in the study is voluntary will also be treated with anonymity. Your interview data will be kept encrypted and confidential. You may withdraw from the study before or during the study by sending me an email at

Data collected during the study will be destroyed by electronic deletion within the legal storage period.

Your participation in the study includes taking part in the prescreening interviews. The purpose of the prescreening interviews is to ensure your eligibility for the study. If selected, you will participate in a 40-55 minutes interviews. Before participation, you will be asked to complete an informed consent form electronically or manually depending on your desire. At the completion of the study, you may request a copy of the study result if you are interested.

Thank you in advance for participating in this study.

Sincerely,

Emmanuel Peter

Dr. Emmanuel Peter is a seasoned leader, a teacher, and counselor. Dr. Peter spent many years helping students in Henrico Public Schools as a teacher. Dr. Peter served as the National President of GIMF (Global Interdenominational Ministers Fellowship). Dr. Peter is currently a GOP candidate for governor in Virginia with the focus on making Virginia a safe place to raise families again. A distinguish Faculty Member of *American Journal of Transformational Leadership (AJTL)*. Dr. Peter holds a doctorate in Management in Organizational Leadership.

 School of Advanced Studies
University of Phoenix

 American Journal *of*
Transformational Leadership